28025

OUR HANDCUFFED POLICE

The Assault upon Law and Order in America and What Can Be Done About It

by EDWARD J. VAN ALLEN

Published by

REPORTORIAL PRESS

Mineola, N. Y.

PRINTED IN THE UNITED STATES OF AMERICA BY
Theo. Gaus' Sons, Inc.
BROOKLYN, N. Y.

CONTENTS

CHAPTER ONE

Anti-Police Brutality

AT 36, plainclothesman Anthony F. Campisi was at the top of the world. He had a loving wife, two children, and a good home in Glendale, New York.

A nine-year veteran of the police force, he was no stranger to the dangers the members of his profession face every day: the sinister assassin lurking in a dark alley, the armed robber who will shoot to kill to protect his own skin, the mild, unobtrusive soul who may suddenly go berserk and kill anyone about him. Campisi probably feared none of these things. Policemen, after all, are realists, fatalistic perhaps, but realists nevertheless.

Yet, plainclothesman Campisi didn't know—he couldn't have—that death lay in waiting for him in the early evening hours of Friday, November 4, 1966, as he went about his admittedly dangerous assignment—helping rid the Times Square, New York City, area of undesirables of many stripes and varieties: purse snatchers, con men, prostitutes, and such lesser lights as the human derelicts with which so many New York City streets abound.

As police pieced the story together later, Campisi had been in the process of arresting a practitioner of the "world's oldest profession" when the prostitute broke away from him. He pursued her, as any good and dutiful policeman would; and then it was that death, swift, sure, and terrible, stole out of the night in an area known as the "crossroads of the world." A man variously described as the "boy friend" and a "pimp" for the woman rounded a corner, a knife flashed in the semi-darkness once, twice, and a courageous policeman fell, mortally wounded in the neck and chest.

For what did such a man as plainclothesman Campisi die? For duty. For country. For upholding the law of this land called America.

The arrest of the suspected perpetrators of this foul murder in the streets of New York, a teeming city which public relations-minded

1

Mayor John V. Lindsay glowingly calls "Fun City," was not long in coming. More than 100 detectives, some of them off-duty volunteers, currycombed the area in search of the killer and his business partner. Armed with descriptions of three witnesses, they soon apprehended a woman and her "boy friend." Both, it turned out, were residents of the Bedford-Stuyvesant section of Brooklyn, which has won unwanted notoriety during the last few years for the high incidence of assorted rapes, assaults, and murders within its environs.

In recent years, the policeman, he who puts his own life on the line in the daily performance of his duties, has been the butt of many charges of "police brutality." Civil rights groups especially have punctuated their protests by parades, demonstrations, sit-ins, and "lie-downs" or "lie-ins." Yet, little has been said about the other side of the coin, the back or black side which demonstrates that the upholder of law and order in America is himself often the victim of brutality, public or "people brutality."

Witness:

● In Jasper County, Iowa, when a marshal tried to arrest a young man, the latter smashed a pop bottle against the side of a building and slashed the marshal's throat with its jagged edges. According to sworn testimony, he then proceeded to "hammer" his victim on the side of the head with a chair. The marshal "bled like a stuck hog," one informed source reported.

Tried for "assault with intent to do great bodily injury," the youngster was acquitted, despite the apparently damaging testimony. The reason, according to one juror: The state didn't prove which one, the officer or the defendant, *had struck the first blow.*

● In Atlanta, Georgia, a Negro detective approached a father to discuss a juvenile-delinquency problem. After the conversation, the father lashed out at the detective. The initial blow shattered the officer's jaw, making a call for help impossible. In desperation, the detective finally drew his gun and shot his assailant in the leg, thereby possibly saving himself from a fatal pounding.

Ironically, the officer was assigned to the Police Department's *helping-hand squad.**

---

* See "Talk About Police Brutality . . ." by Bill Shipp, THE READER'S DIGEST, Oct. 1966, condensed from Sunday Atlanta JOURNAL AND CONSTITUTION.

• In Suffolk County, New York, a stolen-car suspect beat up a patrolman with the officer's own nightstick. The provocation: The officer had merely asked the suspect for his license and registration after the stolen car had been involved in an accident with another vehicle carrying six passengers. Several of the passengers needed medical attention for their injuries. The policeman joined them when he was treated at a hospital for head cuts.

• A New York City policeman who held his fire for fear of hitting passersby in an Easter holiday crowd was stabbed in the hand and thigh and sent to the hospital in critical condition by a suspect wanted in connection with another stabbing.

Unlike other New Yorkers who have witnessed crimes occurring before their eyes without lifting a finger to aid the victim, passersby helped the bleeding policeman subdue the knife-wielder.

• Another New York City policeman had a whole family to contend with when he questioned the age of a young girl ordering a drink in a bar. The mother, also in the bar buying beer, attacked the policeman while the young girl, just 17, ran out to get her two brothers since the family lived nearby. The brothers responded rather heroically. All piled onto the officer, who was smashed over the head with a bar stool by some unidentified participant in the melee. Knocked to the floor, the policeman was beaten and kicked, after which the battling members of the family scurried to their home, a few doors away.

The whole family, including the father, who had barricaded the door to their apartment, was placed under arrest when four patrol cars responded to the urgent call.

The victim of the vicious assault, an officer previously decorated for bravery because he had shot and killed one of four holdup men sticking up a tavern some months before, received eight stitches in his head and five in one finger as a result of the tussle touched off merely by his questioning the age of a girl obviously too young to drink intoxicating beverages.

• In a little East Coast village a husband came home unexpectedly on a Christmas day and found his wife's boy friend in the home. Called to the house, a police officer who sought to prevent the husband from killing his wife (the boy friend had, in the meantime, judiciously disappeared) was himself set upon by the irate husband, who outweighed the policeman by about 60 pounds. As the two tussled, they crashed into a table, which collapsed. Today, over three years later, the officer still suffers from agonizing back pains. His condition has been variously diagnosed as a "back sprain," a "muscle strain," and a "nerve injury."

"Periodic strappings and cortisone are the only things that help kill the pain in my back," the officer says.

Day by day the newspapers chronicle assaults resulting in injury, disability, or death to policemen: the officer killed by a point-blank shotgun blast in the face; the one knocked unconscious and then kicked in the head and body while lying senseless in ten-below-zero weather; the three men who beat a deputy sheriff unconscious when he stopped their car and tried to arrest them; the parents who assaulted a patrolman summoned to the scene after they had assaulted a school principal; the enraged woman driver who bit a policeman after he stopped her for speeding; the young man who attempted to run an officer down with his car after the policeman had stopped the man on a traffic charge.

One could tabulate incident after incident, assault upon assault, murder after murder to the point of ennui in demonstrating how the peace officer, he who is our first line of defense against crime, is frequently the victim of crimes committed by vicious, depraved, sadistic persons who, by accident of birth—and by that single fact alone—are members of the human race.

In addressing ourselves to this subject, the crimes-against-police statistics cited by the Federal Bureau of Investigation in its Uniform Crime Reports for the United States in 1965*speak eloquently, though grimly, for themselves.

● The total of assaults on police officers in the United States during 1965 were 20,523, of which 6,836 were injured.

● A total of 83 officers were killed in the line of duty in 1965. Fifty-three of this number were murdered. The others were killed as a result of accidents.

● From 1960 through 1965, 278 policemen (including city, county, and state police) were killed by felons.

Fifty-eight, or 21 percent, were killed responding to "disturbance calls." Thirty-three, or 12 percent, were killed during burglaries in

---

* Obtainable from the Superintendent of Documents, U. S. Printing Office, Washington, D. C. 20402; price, 55 cents each.

progress or while pursuing burglary suspects. Fifty-five, or 20 percent, were killed while robberies were in progress or while pursuing robbery suspects. Eighty-four, or by and large the greatest percentage (30 percent), were killed while attempting to make arrests or while transporting prisoners. Thirty-one, or 11 percent, were killed investigating suspicious persons and circumstances, while 17, or six percent, were killed by berserk or deranged persons. ("No warning, unprovoked attack," the parenthetical matters reads.)

All but one of the 53 officers murdered in 1965 died from wounds inflicted by firearms: Thirty-two were victims of hand guns; 13 were blasted into oblivion by shotguns; and seven were cut down by rifle fire.

Just as importantly, since 1960 firearms have accounted for 96 percent of the murders of police officers in the line of duty. Of those killed by firearms, 78 percent were murdered by hand guns, showing that that weapon is far and away the favorite in police murder.

Rather ironically, the patrolman acting alone does not appear to be any safer than those who receive assistance. In fact, he appears to be safer, for during the six years these figures cover, 123 officers died while operating alone, while 155 were killed while receiving assistance.

The number of recidivists (habitual or repeat criminals) is also an eye-stopper. "When an examination is made of the prior criminal histories of those involved (in the 278 police murders)," say the Uniform Crime Reports, "it is found that 76 percent had been arrested on some criminal charge prior to the time they became participants in the police murders."

Of even more significance, over one-half of this group had been previously arrested for assaultive-type crimes such as robbery, rape, assault with a deadly weapon, assault with intent to kill, etc. Moreover, the record startlingly discloses that nine persons had been charged at some prior time with the commission of murder.

To indicate how leniency or laxity, however one may put it, on the part of judges contributes to an increase in crime, seven of these nine persons previously charged with murder had been paroled on the charge; one was an escapee from prison, where he was serving time for murder; and the last was an escapee who slipped out of the law's clutches while awaiting trial for murder.

And to further underscore how the courts themselves unwittingly aid and abet the criminal element and help hike the ever-swelling crime rate in the United States, 68 percent of the 362 persons responsible for the 278 police murders are known to have had prior convictions on criminal charges, and *more than two-thirds* of this group had received "kid-glove" or "slap-on-the-wrist" treatment from the courts by way of being placed on probation or being paroled on at least one of their prior convictions.

Astoundingly, more than one of every four of the murderers of police officers were either on parole or on probation when they committed the ultimate of crimes.

The age range of police murderers—from a boy of 14 to a septuagenarian (73)—is also of surpassing interest. All told, 17 of the slayers were under 18, 40 were in the 18-20 group, and 99, by far the biggest percentage, were in the 21-25 age bracket. A total of 22 were over 50 years of age when they murdered a police officer.

Most peace officer killers lie in the 20-30 age span, while 25 appears to be the age when the man intent on murder is more likely to end the life of a policeman.

Paradoxically, relatives or friends, not strangers as popularly thought, constitute the greatest threat to the potential victim of crime. According to the Uniform Crime Reports, about 70 percent of all wilful killings, nearly two-thirds of all aggravated assaults, and a goodly percentage of forcible rapes are committed by family members, friends, or other persons known at some time to their victims. Robbery alone is the exception. The stranger is more likely to rob you than is a relative or friend. Policemen, however, generally are strangers to their killers. (This matter is just touched upon here. National crime statistics will be treated with more fully in a later chapter.)

Do statistics like these instill and infuse a sense of shame in American citizens? Do they anger, arouse, or even disturb the conscience of a people who appear to be too "uncitizenly," if we may coin a word, or even, perhaps, a bit too cowardly to speak for an ordered and orderly society at a time when the freaks of this land, the unkept, uncombed, unwashed, uncouth beatniks, peaceniks, beardniks, and just plain anti-policeniks spit in the eye of the law? Or at a time when constantly climbing crime is a national disgrace of unparalleled proportions?

Self-answering questions like these need no further comment. If you would like other answers, though, I suggest you

Ask the grieving relatives of policemen killed by vermin who periodically come out of their human ratholes to attack, maim, or brutally murder the front-line fighter for law and order in America.

Or ask the family of the Suffolk County, New York, policeman paralyzed from the waist down as a result of a gun battle with an accused wife beater.

Or ask the neighbors and friends and the assistant district attorney who conducted a drive to sell 500 dinner tickets to aid the family of this paralyzed policeman.

Or go even further: Ask this disabled peace officer's six children who relied on their father for sustenance why their father, whose shield they undoubtedly regarded as a badge of honor, has suddenly been hopelessly disabled.

Ask them. Through their tears, you may get some answers.

Better still, address yourself to the question of law and order in the United States and ask yourself this question:

Which side am I on, the side of lawlessness or the side of the law-abiding American who cares for his country, reveres its institutions, and cherishes its freedoms, which he fully knows carry with them one simple burden: that of good citizenship?

CHAPTER TWO

Duties of the Police

"WE TOLD PEOPLE, 'This is an emergency—everybody out!' No one argued."

There was a certain matter-of-factness, almost a touch of non-chalance, implicit in the statement as New York City Patrolman Francis D. P. Keating described how he and brother Patrolman John J. O'Connor spotted the sure signs of impending disaster when they investigated a reported gas leak in a section of Jamaica, Queens.

The two officers, the first on the scene, made one of those split-second decisions which in other situations have at times triggered charges of "police brutality." Hearing a "tremendous noise," an ominous rumbling, Patrolman O'Connor turned in the first alarm at 5:19 A. M. on Friday, January 13, 1967, just nine minutes after the first report of the gas leak was telephoned in by a worried resident.

Once the alarm summoning help was given, the two officers rushed from house to house telling people still fog-eyed with sleep to get out without bothering to take anything with them.

Four other patrolmen and a dozen firemen were next on the scene, the firemen in two engines which were to become casualties of the fire. The gas was so thick, so heavy in the street at that time that the fire engines simply stalled from lack of oxygen.

"The hell with the engines. Let's get the people," Fire Lieutenant Thomas Egan reportedly yelled.

And get the people they did. Bewildered, many of them uncertain as to exactly what was happening, people poured out of their threatened homes in nightgowns, pajamas, overcoats, undershorts. Some even were shoeless. Converging on the scene in increasing numbers, other policemen commandered cars and trucks to evacuate the residents from the area posthaste.

It was between the second and third fire alarms that the explosion came. Like a volcano blowing its top, the fire surged from the ground and shot skyward in a towering column of flame that ate its way as

8

much as 200 feet in the air. The resultant mountain of fire and smoke could be seen at least 25 miles away.

Three two-family wooden and brick buildings, cleared of their occupants scant minutes before, were almost instantly leveled to burning heaps. As though expressing contempt for fire, the element with which they were so familiar, two lone chimneys still stood, mutely evidencing the presence of buildings which now no longer existed.

All told, the flames rolled through a six-block area, engulfing nine homes and severly damaging eight others before firemen, responding to a total of 13 alarms, brought the fire under control.

Thus were hundreds of persons saved from serious injury or death by the quick thinking and fast action of two policemen who correctly assessed imminent disaster and risked their own lives to save a huge number of fellow citizens who, on that particular Friday morning, had been blissfully unaware of their nearness to eternity.

And on that same morning when a major miracle took place in Jamaica, New York, both firemen and police echoed one another's sentiments when they were heard to say:

"I'll never understand how nobody was killed. Thank God."

Officers Keating and O'Connor were heroized, and rightly so. Yet, what they did was simply to react speedily in accordance with their duties as police officers. They had a split-second decision to make, and fortunately it paid tremendous dividends in human lives.

Fire fighting is not, of course, the policeman's lot. Nevertheless, because one of his main functions is patrol, he is often the first to discover a fire, the first to turn in an alarm, and the first to rescue persons from burning buildings. Such cases are numberless, as are instances in which policemen have administered life-saving first aid, mouth-to-mouth breathing, etc. before ambulances and expert medical help have arrived at the scene of a fire.

Controlling people's behavior at fires is a collaterally important duty of the policeman. A 13-alarmer may, as the Jamaica fire did, attract thousands of spectators who must be cordoned off and kept away from the fire fighting and rescue operations in progress. At the same time, traffic must be routed or rerouted around the area of the fire, emergency vehicles responding to the scene must not be impeded by "gawkers" blocking the road, etc.

Fires large or small, life-taking and property-damaging or minor, are not the sole and only concern of the police officer. Traffic safety is always his concern, and it does not simply entail writing summonses for driving or other traffic infractions. A policeman or policemen are usually called to the scene of a traffic accident, especially one involving death or injury to life and property. Once there, the officer initially responding, thus usually in charge, must get the names and addresses of the drivers and any injured persons, must summon medical help if needed, and must later file detailed accident reports describing what happened, who was involved, and what action was taken. During this time traffic must be kept flowing past or around the scene of the accident, matters with which most citizens are familiar, but which are nevertheless sufficiently important to be touched upon here.

Concerned as he is with traffic safety and with reducing the carnage on the highways, the policeman often runs traffic safety schools for motorists and pedestrians alike. In Cleveland the police have conducted lectures, have shown films, and have answered questions of senior citizen groups whose members are prone to have accidents, particularly the concededly unequal pedestrian-versus-vehicle type.

Most citizens are familiar with the "Walk," "Don't Walk" signs used at traffic controlled intersections in some cities in an effort to prevent jaywalkers from taking their lives in their hands by ambling or strolling into moving traffic when common sense would dictate otherwise.

Police in some areas have augmented such devices by running "pedestrian schools" to which pedestrian violators are invited. There the "students" hear lectures on pedestrian safety on today's traffic-choked roads.

Besides his concern with traffic safety, the police officer is often-times called when there are accidents in the home, explosions in the home or in factories, to the scene of other types of industrial disasters, etc.—in short, in almost any type of emergency in which fast, competent, sometimes life-saving assistance is demanded, the policeman is summoned.

If people are likely to injure or kill themselves in the home, some-times through such senseless means as leaving a roller skate on a stairway, they are just as wont to hurt themselves or invite death via the water-sport route. In the United States more than 6,000 persons drown yearly. They drown while swimming, they fall off boats, they fall off docks, embankments, etc.

That the drowning need not be in a lake, a bay, or the body of water, but may even be in a bathtub merely points up the careless-ness of some people in their ordinary, everyday living habits.

There are many cases on record in which policemen have used mouth-to-mouth breathing to revive persons who had "drowned," thereby saving their lives long before fire departments, rescue squads, or ambulances with resuscitators or inhalators arrived.

In *The Policeman's Manual*,* Captain Carl Vollmer of the New York City Police Department lists the duties of policemen, as set forth in the New York City Charter, in simple tabular form:

1. Preserve the peace.
2. Protect life and property.
3. Prevent crime.
4. Enforcement of all laws and ordinances.
5. Detect and arrest offender.

These duties are necessarily interrelated. As a matter of fact, in arresting a particular offender or suspect, the policeman may actually be performing all five functions at once.

As this New York City Charter police-duty blueprint in thumb-nail form tends to underscore, people usually regard the policeman as a law enforcer primarily. In reality, law enforcement, while a major function, is just one of many that the police officer performs. Besides those already discussed, other duties include:

Assisting stranded motorists.

Watching polls on Election Day.

Licensing taxicabs and bicycles.

Operating animal shelters (in some police jurisdictions).

Rescuing lost children. (Who has not seen newspaper pictures of policemen feeding ice cream to little lost souls too tiny to know where they live?)

Responding to medical emergencies such as heart attacks, strokes, etc.

Appearing in court to testify in accident cases and to testify against arrested persons and persons to whom summonses for traffic violations have been issued.

Many persons believe the police officer should be relieved of all duties not directly related to what may be considered his chief duty, that of law enforcement. In that connection, who has not heard of

---

* Published by Arco Publishing Company.

the motorist who tartly told an officer, while receiving a highly un-welcome ticket: "Why aren't you out arresting *real* criminals?"

People on both sides of this question as to whether the police should be freed of all duties except the principal one of enforcing the law advance rather weighty arguments. One side claims that police-men cannot deter, detect, or solve crimes while engaged in such relatively minor duties as traffic control. The other side argues with equal vehemence that policemen often do prevent or even solve crimes by virtue of being present and available when needed.

There is no doubt that the mere presence of a policeman in a given area is at least a partial deterrent to crime. I would go so far as to venture the opinion that if it were possible to have one police-man for every block in the nation (probably 20 million officers, a manifest impossibility, of course), crime could be wiped out virtually overnight.

As it is, we must rely on the policeman's cardinal function in the area of crime prevention, actual, preferably around-the-clock patrol of our streets, whether by car or on foot.

There are ways in which we the people can help make the patrol-man more efficient in making his never-ending rounds. Those will be taken up in a later chapter, as will some other important police func-tions such as investigation, research, and detection techniques.

While the police officer is involved in such mundane matters as promoting public safety, it is his job as a crime fighter, his attempts at protecting the public as much as is humanly possible from criminals with the means at his disposal, that both attract the most public attention and draw the most fire from critics and actual enemies of law enforcement in America.

The Supreme Court of the United States, while not classifiable as an out-and-out "enemy" of the police in this land, is nevertheless an all-powerful critic of the police and how they work. The continuing tendency of the Supreme Court to lay down rules and regulations as to how the policeman may comport himself in making arrests and in uncovering evidence of crime has given birth to a furor not likely to completely abate in our time.

CHAPTER THREE

Manacling the Police

JOSE SUAREZ stood before the bar of justice in a Brooklyn, New York, courtroom. Outwardly unemotional, he appeared almost uninterested in the proceedings in which he was *the* central figure.

At 23, the comparatively small and slight Suarez was a rather remarkable man. Still, few would envy him, few would willingly share the burden of his conscience; for this inoffensive-looking 23-year-older was confessor to the slaying of his wife and their five small children.

There was more than a hint of displeasure in the voice of Supreme Court Justice Michael Kern as he sat in his high-backed chair behind the bench and looked down at the defendant.

"Judges are bound," Judge Kern observed with a note of regret, "by many decisional laws with which they don't agree.

"Even an animal such as this one—and I think it would be insulting the animal kingdom—must be clothed with all these safeguards. This is a very sad thing. It is repulsive. It makes any human being's blood run cold and his stomach turn to let a thing like this out in the streets."

Nevertheless, that is precisely what Justice Kern did. That is precisely what he was bound to do; the Supreme Court of the United States had so decreed.

Thus was one Jose Suarez once again turned loose because, although he had admitted the fatal stabbing of his wife and five children ranging in age from 11 months to five years, his constitutional rights had not been fully protected in accordance with the fiat of the U. S. Supreme Court.

It wasn't that the state didn't want to prosecute this man. It wasn't that society itself didn't demand full and final retribution for the murder of six defenseless souls. Oh, no. It was simply that it couldn't prosecute the accused by virtue of the precedential decision handed down by the U. S. Supreme Court in the case of Ernesto A. Miranda against the State of Arizona, to be discussed below.

The state actually had nothing on Suarez beyond his police station confession in the presence of an assistant district attorney. But the confession had a flaw in it, a vital flaw all-important to Suarez. The district attorney readily admitted that the defendant had not been apprised of his rights *before* he confessed the mass slayings.

Significantly, Suarez' confession was in April, 1966, while the Miranda decision which was to set him free in February, 1967, was handed down by the U. S. Supreme Court in June, 1966.

More than anything else the Suarez case demonstrated the importance of a suspect's confession in the absence of any other evidence pointing to his guilt. Said Assistant District Attorney Nathan R. Schor: "With a heavy heart, I am reluctantly constrained at this point to move for dismissal of this indictment. The district attorney has no other evidence but the confession."

This spectacular scene of a man being freed despite having confessed to man's greatest crime against his fellow man has been and is being repeated throughout the country.

In another case, this time in Queens County, New York, a manslaughter indictment aaginst a 22-year-old man charged with beating and kicking a union official to death was thrown out because, while the police had advised the man of his rights, they simply hadn't gone far enough. The detectives who had arrested the suspect said they had advised him of all his constitutional rights, including his right to remain mute and his right to have an attorney present during any questioning. The defendant was taken to the station house and a call was made to his lawyer. Learning that the lawyer was in court on another matter, the police left word that he should call them back.

Shortly thereafter, the defendant was asked if he would submit to a lie-detector test. He acquiesced and was taken to Manhattan for purposes of the test.

Soon after the departure of the officers and the defendant, the attorney called. Told the suspect was not available, he informed the police that he didn't want his client questioned any further. The lawyer then journeyed to the station house, where he repeated his request. But before word could be gotten to the detectives accompanying the defendant, the suspect had made a statement without the use of the lie detector.

New York State Supreme Court Justice J. Irwin Shapiro, likewise complying with the dictates of the decision in the Miranda case, ruled that the people had "failed to sustain the 'heavy' burden which rests upon them of demonstrating an intelligent and knowing waiver by the defendant at the time he made the statement in question.

"It may well be," the judge said, "that the defendant would have refused to talk to the police in the absence of his attorney had he known that his attorney had instructed the police not to question the defendant."

And so it was that the state yet again set a man free because it found the police hadn't fully protected the suspect's constitutional rights.

The spectacle of accuseds who had confessed major crimes being freed without so much as a slap on the wrist is not peculiar to New York State. Similar travesties on justice are being repeated and re-enacted all over the nation as lower court judges, some of them shaking their heads in tacit disagreement with a decision which is a mandate to them, let confessors to man's gravest crime go un-punished by a society which is perhaps a bit too beneficent and benevolent for its own good.

Judge for yourself:

● A 21-year-old man who had admitted raping a 71-year-old woman was released by an appellate court. The reason: He had not been advised of his constitutional rights to remain silent and to have a lawyer when he was taken into custody in March, 1965.

● Another appellate court threw out a manslaughter conviction on the ground that the lower court had erred in allowing the de-fendant's confession to be received in evidence during his trial. Why? "At the time the defendant was without counsel and had not been informed of his rights," the appellate court ruled.

● Probably classic among cases of this kind is that of 41-year-old James W. Killough who on three separate occasions voluntarily confessed killing his wife and throwing her body on a dump.

In directing the acquittal of the defendant, Federal Judge George L. Hart angrily told a Washington, D. C., jury: ". . . the U. S. Court of Appeals has seen fit to throw the confessions out. Though it makes me almost physically ill, I must direct a verdict of acquittal. I feel I'm presiding not over a search for truth, but over an impossible farce. We know the man is guilty, but we sit here blind, deaf, and dumb, and we can't admit what we know. Tonight felons can sleep better."

What is this Miranda decision which in effect gives confessors to murder and perpetrators of other crimes license to prey upon society all over again?

To fully understand Miranda and its implications, it is best to narrate precisely what happened in that case.

On March 3, 1963, an 18-year-old girl was kidnapped and forcibly raped near Phoenix, Arizona. Ten days later, on the morning of March 13, a man named Ernesto A. Miranda was arrested and taken to the police station. At this time Miranda was 23 years old, indigent, and educated to the extent of having completed half the ninth grade. He had an "emotional illness" of the schizophrenic type, according to the doctor who eventually examined him. The doctor's report also stated that Miranda was "alert and oriented as to time, place, and person," intelligent within normal limits, competent to stand trial, and sane within the legal definition.

At the police station, the victim picked Miranda out of a lineup, and two officers then took him into a separate room to interrogate him, starting about 11:30 A. M. Though at first denying his guilt, within a short time Miranda gave a detailed oral confession and then wrote out in his own hand and signed a brief statement admitting and describing the crime.

All this was accomplished in two hours or less without any force, threats, or promises.

At his trial in an Arizona State court, Miranda's confession was admitted in evidence; and he was convicted of kidnapping and rape. On appeal, the Arizona Supreme Court affirmed or held that the conviction was proper.

But in a hair-splitting, sharply divided five-to-four decision, the Supreme Court of the United States reversed Miranda's conviction.

Holding that the confession had been inadmissible because Miranda had not been in any way apprised of his right to counsel or of his privilege against self-incrimination, the highest court in this land laid down four rules which the police must follow in dealing with suspects during "custodial interrogation." They are that prior to any questioning, the person

1. Must be warned that he has a right to remain silent.
2. Must be warned that any statement he does make may be used as evidence against him.

3. Must be told he has a right to the presence of an attorney, either retained or appointed.

4. May waive effectuation of the other three rights, provided the waiver is made *voluntarily, knowingly, and intelligently*.

Speaking for the five-man majority, Chief Justice Earl Warren went further. He said: "If, however, he (the defendant) indicates in any manner or at any stage of the process that he wishes to consult with an attorney before speaking, there can be no questioning. Likewise, if the defendant is alone and indicates in any manner that he does not wish to be interrogated, the police may not question him. The mere fact that he may have answered some questions or volunteered some statements on his own does not deprive him of the right to refrain from answering any further inquiries until he has consulted with an attorney and thereafter consents to be questioned."

Quite understandably, the broader, hence more liberal, interpretation by the five-man majority of the protection against self-incrimination provided by the Fifth Amendment to the Constitution of the United States drew some rather stinging dissents from the four-man minority.

In accusing the majority of going "too far too fast," Associate Justice Clark declared: "Custodial interrogation has long been recognized as 'undoubtedly an essential tool of law enforcement.'" He contended that the "totality of circumstances" in each case should be the rule in determining whether a confession of an accused is voluntary. He said he would "consider in each case whether the police officer prior to custodial interrogation added the warning that the suspect might have counsel present at the interrogation and, further, that a court would appoint one at his request if he was too poor to employ counsel. In the absence of warnings, the burden would be on the State to prove that counsel was knowingly and intelligently waived or that in the totality of circumstances, including the failure to give the necessary warnings, the confession was clearly voluntary."

Speaking for brother dissenters, Justices Stewart and White, Mr. Justice Harlan was almost caustically critical of the five-man majority. He wrote: "I believe the decision of the Court represents poor constitutional law and *entails harmful consequences for the country at large*. How serious these consequences may prove to be only time can tell." (Emphasis supplied.)

(Tolling time has already told quite a story, with an incalculable number of accuseds being freed because the police had only their confessions to go on. Also, an indeterminable number of persons already convicted have been let go because their convictions were based on confessions taken by police without following, virtually syllable by syllable, the Supreme Court's mandate as to spelling out a suspect's constitutional rights.)

Mr. Justice Harlan continued: "How much harm this decision will inflict on law enforcement cannot fairly be predicted with accuracy. Evidence on the role of confessions is notoriously incomplete . . . We do know that *some crimes cannot be solved without confessions,* that ample expert testimony attests to their importance in crime control, and that the Court is taking a real risk with society's welfare in imposing its new regime on the country. The social costs of crime are too great to call the new rules anything but a hazardous experimentation."

In a separate dissent, Mr. Justice White made a particularly startling statement: "And this Court," he said, "has left standing literally thousands of criminal convictions that rested at least in part on confessions taken in the course of interrogation by the police after arrest."

Justice White's exception-taking word raise an intriguing question: If the majority's opinion is correct as to Miranda and the three other cases decided by the court at the same time and is applicable to cases occurring *after* Miranda, why isn't it equally applicable to all such cases, whether they took place a year ago, five years ago, or 10 or more years ago? Aren't all felons entitled to stand equal under the law?

It is this writer's considered opinion that even the all-powerful Supreme Court of the United States wouldn't dare dictate that its historic decision be fairly and equally applied to all cases in which convictions were gotten based on confessions taken from defendants without a point-by-point, sentence-by-sentence, and word-by-word forewarning of their constitutional rights and a proper "voluntary, knowing, and intelligent" waiver of those rights.

Why wouldn't it so dare? Simply because most of the jails in the country would be suddenly emptied.

Mr. Justice White took issue with the Supreme Court majority in other vital respects. Said he:

"The most basic function of any government is to provide for the security of the individual and of his property. These ends of society are served by the criminal laws which for the most part are aimed at the prevention of crime. Without the reasonably effective performance of the task of preventing private violence and retaliation, it is idle to talk about human dignity and civilized values."

He went on to say that the criminal laws "serve the interest in general security" in many ways: by removing the murderer from the streets, thereby preventing repetitions of his offense; by discouraging the temptation to commit crime in those who may see their own neighbor swiftly and surely apprehended should he commit a crime; and by attempting, sometimes successfully, at times unsuccessfully, to return the convict to society a better and more law-abiding man than when he entered prison to pay for his crime or crimes.

Direly Justice White predicted: "In some unknown number of cases the Court's rule will return a killer, a rapist or other criminal to the streets and to the environment which produced him, to repeat his crime whenever it pleases him."

The real concern, he added, lies in the "impact on those who rely on the public authority for protection and who without it can only engage in violent self-help with guns, knives, and the help of their neighbors similarly inclined." Then with an unmistakable touch of sarcasm, he said: "There is, of course, a saving factor: the next victims are uncertain, unnamed, and unrepresented in this case."

That Americans are indeed increasingly turning to ways to protect themselves because of the inability of the shackled police to cope with ever-burgeoning crime in the United States will be detailed in a later chapter.

Suffice to say that the four dissenters to the majority opinion of the U. S. Supreme Court in Miranda foresaw an inevitable increase in crime in this country directly as a result of that decision.

Unless the court itself modifies the stiff requirements which effectively handcuff the police insofar as evidence gathered by way of confession is concerned, the furious reaction to the Miranda decision is certain to seethe for many years. In fact, in the majority decision the court itself took cognizance of the expected reaction to the serious restrictions on police seeking to solve crimes by the confession method. In a footnote, it cited the words of the late Los Angeles Police Chief W. H. Parker, who charged that the court was opening up a whole "Pandora's box" as to "under what circumstances" a defendant could "intelligently waive" his constitutional rights. "Allegations that modern criminal investigation can compensate for the lack of a confession or admission in every criminal case are totally absurd," Parker declared.

The freeing of persons accused of capital and other crimes since the Miranda decision made legal history on June 13, 1966, thus far bears out the accuracy of Police Chief Parker's comments. Suarez was freed because the police had not a scintilla of evidence beyond the man's own confession to rely on. And the accused in the kicking and beating manslaughter case was freed because, as the court said, he had not made an "intelligent and knowing waiver" of his constitutional rights before he gave his statement to the police.

Another deputy chief of police from a Southern city, who declined to be quoted directly, said of the Miranda case: "They (the U. S. Supreme Court) are going all out to protect the criminal element and disregarding 95 percent of the citizens who are law-abiding."

A sampling of the opinion of other police chiefs around the country shows that many agree that the U. S. Supreme Court has placed the criminal in a privileged position, leaving the bemused victim of crime and the criminal even more unprotected than he ever was in that it makes the prosecution and conviction of persons accused of crimes more difficult than ever and impossible in some cases.

Is any further proof needed that the U. S. Supreme Court is actually fostering crime when it coddles the criminal, penalizes his victims, and shackles the police in their efforts to prevent crime and to insure the apprehension of its perpetrators?

The police, understandably prejudiced in their own behalf, are not alone in looking askance at the Supreme Court's decision. Since Miranda, the law journals of various universities in the United States have been replete with articles discussing the pros and cons of that historic decision.

Writing in the December, 1966, Fordham University Law Review, U. S. Sixth Circuit Court of Appeals Judge George Edwards said: ". . . I believe this case (Miranda) will have a real effect on law enforcement.

"In some cases it will make identification and conviction more difficult."

The judge, a former police commissioner of the City of Detroit, noted that the police "in their daily confrontation with violent crime both need and deserve the support of the public and the legal profession."

The judge expressed certainty that police practices in the interrogation of criminal suspects in recent years "have markedly improved." Rather singularly, he ventured the opinion that even a person being questioned on the street would be technically in "detention" and thus would have to be warned of his constitutional rights, especially if any prolonged questioning were undertaken.

Writing in the same Law Journal, another critic, Richard H. Kuh, a member of the New York Bar and a former member of the New York County District Attorney's office, contended that there is no such thing as an "intelligent waiver" of one's rights against self-incrimination. He said that the suspect who intentionally hurts himself by confessing is not intelligent at all.

Other lawyers have pointed out that the police themselves should not have to act as judges or lawyers in handing out advice to defendants. On that subject Judge Nathan Sobel of New York had some rather pungent remarks. Said he: The "advice from the police to the kind of illiterate half-wits we see in the Criminal Courts can hardly take the place of advice from one's own lawyer."

A partial answer to that observation is the proposal that lawyers be planted in police stations ready at a second's notice to advise suspects to "Keep your mouth shut."

Other critics call for amending the Fifth Amendment, that which says that no person "shall be compelled in any criminal case to be a witness against himself." Their proposed amendment would place a duty on accused persons to answer questions under proper safeguards, with or without an attorney being present. The amendment proponents also suggest that the failure of any defendant to respond to questions be freely commented upon at the trial by the prosecution and the court.

Perhaps the most valid criticism of the Supreme Court of the United States in its campaign to protect the criminal at all costs, while disregarding the victim of wanton criminality, is the charge that the court is not simply a "national police force" policing the local police, but is actually a new national legislature usurping the legislative prerogatives of the Congress and the legislatures of the respective states.

How does the Supreme Court "legislate" rather than make simple judicial determinations in passing on the convictions of the U. S. residents? When the august Supreme Court of the United States not only decrees that a particular defendant was improperly convicted, but also sets forth rules and regulations that the police must follow in handling suspects, it is in effect "policing the police" and "laying down the law" as to how the police may act in given situations. That is clearly exercising powers which the court does not possess; and it is, in and of itself, in this writer's opinion, an unconstitutional act by the Supreme Court of the United States. In short, the very court which has said that "the police must obey the law while enforcing the law" should look to its own skirts.

In essence, the court may declare a particular law or action unconstitutional, but it may not "enact" laws which it tacitly claims come within the framework of the Constitution. That function, the passing of laws governing the activities of the various instrumentalities of government, is undisputably the province of the respective legislatures of this country.

In a word, the Supreme Court has no right to police the police. Yet that is patently what it is doing. It has no right to pre-empt the legislative function. But that is exactly what it is doing.

Concededly, the respective legislatures have been lax in not having adopted clear rules and regulations prescribing what the police may or may not do in attempting to get suspects to confess. But I fail to see how the Supreme Court of the United States can right a wrong by itself committing a wrong. And nowhere in the U. S. Constitution do I find any grant of the legislative power to the U. S. Supreme Court. On the contrary, the Constitution itself plainly and unequivocally sets forth the distinctions, the rights, the powers, and the prerogatives of each of the three branches of government, the executive, the legislative, and the judicial.

Surely, the legislatures of the respective states could enact—and should enact—proper rules and regulations to be used as blueprints for action by local police.

Congress itself could clip the wings or curb the powers of the U. S. Supreme Court, if it chose to do so. Article III, Section 2, of the U. S. Constitution gives Congress the power to restrict the powers of the court when it says that the court may be subject to "exceptions" and "regulations" of the Congress with respect to the court's appellate jurisdiction.

Congress, though, has never seen fit to curb the appellate powers of the U. S. Supreme Court, demonstrating that it has greater respect for that body than is true in reverse.

Nonetheless, Chief Justice Warren himself has urged legislative action to establish guidelines which the police may follow. In the face of that admission, one wonders why the court has usurped the legislative function by itself "enacting" guidelines which the police must follow.

Adverting once more to Miranda, Mr. Justice Warren and the other four members constituting the majority clearly "took judicial notice" of various interrogation techniques, some involving psychological trickery, set forth in police manuals. In describing these techniques, the majority neither stated nor implied that any of them were used in extracting confessions from Miranda and the other three persons whose cases the court ruled on at the same time. On the contrary, as pointed out by Mr. Justice Harlan in his minority dissent, the confessions were "obtained during brief, daytime questioning conducted by two officers and unmarked by any of the traditional indicia of coercion."

What makes the majority's reliance on police manual "evidence" especially astounding to me is that during more than a quarter century of court and shorthand reporting I don't think I have ever seen a trial court judge who would admit in evidence such patently irrelevant, yet highly inflammatory, material not even remotely connected with the cases at bar.

For a certainty, it may be argued that the Supreme Court of the United States, a dynasty unto itself, is not bound by any ordinary rules of evidence which the court itself does not make. Rules of evidence apparently are for lower courts, not for the SUPREME Court which has a "king can do no wrong" attitude.

One sample of the kind of police manual-outlined technique which the court took cognizance of though it bore absolutely no relation to the cases before it will suffice.

The technique, described rather fully by the majority, is known as the "friendly-unfriendly" or "Mutt and Jeff" act. Two agents or officers are used, Mutt, "the relentless investigator who knows the subject is guilty and is not going to waste any time." Jeff, in contrast, is pictured as a kind-hearted soul, a family man. He "disapproves" of Mutt and his tactics and will arrange to get him off the case if the subject will cooperate. Jeff admits he can't hold Mutt off very long. The subject, he says, would be wise to make a quick decision.

Both men are present while Mutt, the odious one, acts out his role. Jeff may stand by quietly and object from time to time to some of

Mutt's tactics. After Mutt departs the room, Jeff makes his plea for "cooperation." If the plot works, he gets in the form of a confession.

Again to make a concession, few people—including the members of the U. S. Supreme Court—know what goes on in police interrogation rooms, so why shouldn't the court rely on guesswork? Why shouldn't it indeed? Why shouldn't all lawyers, including those on the Supreme Court bench, be bound by evidence, not surmise or mere speculation?

But the Supreme Court of the United States has spoken in the case of Miranda and the lower courts plus the respective police departments of the nation have harkened to its fiats.

Heeding the court's indirect, though binding, directions, police departments in various cities, such as in Topeka, Kansas, have adopted the printed card method of advising suspects of their rights.

The statement the Topeka policeman must read to every suspect is as follows: "I am required by the Constitution to warn you that anything you say may be used against you in a court of law; that you need say nothing and have a right to remain silent. That if you wish you have the right to consult with an attorney and have him present that if you are unable to afford an attorney, one will be appointed for you."

Dr. Kenneth McFarland, architect of *The Topeka Plan for Law Enforcement*, expresses dismay at forcing the police "to go through that preposterous reading exercise with all the drunks, punks, con men, thieves, prostitutes, perverts, and panhandlers they may have reason to suspect, as well as anyone they actually catch red-handed in the most serious of crimes."

The card, though written in the plainest of language, may not be as foolproof as the police think. One must remember that any waiver of rights, even by one ostensibly properly informed of those rights, must be "voluntarily, knowingly, and intelligently" made. What is to stop even the least sophisticated defendant who nevertheless has been "educated" by the Supreme Court of the United States in what his rights are (there are more "jailhouse lawyers" in this country than anyone could possibly count) from coming into court and declaring that he didn't know what he was doing when he waived his rights? After all, the courts themselves, despite what psychologists may claim, have no accurate yardstick for the measurement of human intelligence. And isn't the suspect, as Mr. Kuh has suggested, rather unintelligent

f he willingly confesses to a crime in the face of the fact that his con-
ession is bound to hurt him?

As a further example, the person who "voluntarily and knowingly"
onfesses to a crime to make peace with his own conscience might be
eld not to have made an "intelligent" confession. On the other hand,
et us assume a suspect is subnormal in intelligence anyway. Is he to
o scot-free because he's intellectually incapable of making an "intelli-
ent" confession?

Hailed and denounced on all sides, the Miranda decision must
evertheless be lived with. The police must, as many departments al-
eady have, adapt themselves to it. It is, after all, but the most recent
n a whole series of decisions by which the U. S. Supreme Court has
ffectively diluted the power of the police to enforce the law and
hereby cut the constantly climbing crime rate which makes so many
Americans afraid to walk the streets in the dark of night.

Ironically, Ernesto Miranda, the man who unwittingly has set so
nany confessors to capital and other crimes free, was found guilty of
idnap and rape at the end of his second trial on those charges—de-
pite the inadmissibility of his confession.

And while the original Miranda ruling by the U. S. Supreme Court
vas a landmark decision of astounding repercussive force, it was but
he latest in a whole line of cases liberalizing the approach to criminal
rosecution in the United States. A short history of some of those
ases follows:

Before 1932, when the U. S. Supreme Court ruled that defendants
n a capital case, that of the seven Scottsboro boys who had been
ondemned to death for rape, were entitled to counsel, the Supreme
Court had been reluctant to interfere in any state criminal proceed-
ngs.

Then in 1936 there came before it the appeal of a Negro whose
onfession had been induced by a prolonged whipping with a leather
trap with buckles on it. Facing up to the fact that the due process of
aw doctrine was meaningless to the ordinary citizen, the court as-
umed appellate jurisdiction and overruled the Supreme Court of
Mississippi which had not seen fit to disturb the conviction patently
ased on a coerced confession.

(Parenthetically, I don't believe any responsible police officer
vould characterize beating a suspect to the point of forcing him to
onfess as proper police procedure.)

At any rate, that case, *Brown v. Mississippi** is important in that it actually laid the foundation for Miranda 30 years later.

Other rulings which were to directly or indirectly hamper the police in their work were to follow. In *Spano v. New York,* a first-degree murder case, the U. S. Supreme Court held that a confession coerced from a prisoner without any physical brutality, but by means of what the court termed "official pressure, fatigue, and sympathy falsely aroused" was inadmissible under "due process" standards.

In *Malloy v. Hogan** the court departed from long-established precedent and held that the Fifth Amendment privilege of silence enjoyed by an accused is part of the due process right which the states must observe.

*Escobedo v. Illinois*** was the immediate forerunner of Miranda. In that case the court ordered a new trial for the defendant because, while he had had a lawyer present at the scene, he was not warned of his rights to counsel and silence and was repeatedly denied the opportunity to see his lawyer prior to confessing.

Other legal stumbling blocks have been tossed in front of policemen seeking to do their duty. Up to 1961 the police were pretty much free to operate without search warrants because the U. S. Supreme Court hadn't interfered with state courts' rights to rule on the admissibility of evidence obtained through search and seizure without a warrant.

But in 1961, the Cleveland police, acting on a tip, broke into the home of a woman named Dollree Mapp.*** They were looking for a bombing suspect and a "large amount of policy paraphernalia." They found neither, so they put handcuffs on the woman and continued their search. Eventually they found a batch of "obscene materials," for the possession of which Dollree Mapp was arrested and subsequently convicted.

In upholding her appeal, the Supreme Court ruled that every state must obey the "exclusionary rule," meaning that state courts must exclude from evidence anything obtained through unreasonable searches and seizures.

Other rulings have slowly but surely gnawed away the power of the police to do their duty in protecting the victims of crime by ap-

---

* 297 U. S. 287, 282 (1936).
* *Malloy v. Hogan,* 378 U. S. 1 (1964).
** *Escobedo v. Illinois,* 378 U. S. 478 (1964).
*** *Mapp v. Ohio,* 367 U. S. 643 (1961).

prehending those who commit the crimes. Right now, as this book is being written, the constitutionality of New York State's "stop and frisk" law is under attack before the U. S. Supreme Court. In two actions, one by a man charged with possession of burglar's tools, the other by a person allegedly in possession of narcotics, the law is being challenged on the ground that the suspects have been the victims of an unreasonable search and seizure.

If the U. S. Supreme Court's past performances are any criteria, the court is likely to hold that the suspects' Fourth Amendment rights have in fact been violated; and in that event, New York's "stop and frisk" law will be tossed into a legal trashcan.

In that case, the power of the police to arrest a man on suspicion because he is seen furtively lugging a heavy suitcase through the streets in the wee hours may likewise be abridged. As a matter of fact, in one such case a patrolman who stopped such a man and took him to the station house for interrogation was later taken to task despite the fact that the suitcase was found to contain burglarized articles. In dismissing the case, the court ruled the arrest was unlawful because the officer didn't know at the time he accosted and detained the defendant that a burglary had actually been committed.

Is it any wonder that some policemen say, as one told me not too long ago, "Why should we arrest anybody? The courts will only let him go."

Confronted with a steady stream of cases effectively frustrating the police, if not actually handcuffing them, what conclusion is the ordinary citizen to draw except that crime is on the upgrade in this country because law enforcement is being pushed downhill by the courts themselves?

For their part, policemen want to do their duty under the law. They want to obey that law, as the Supreme Court has said they should. Semi-military in character, police departments are, for the most part, peopled by professionals who know their job and are skilled in carrying it out. Yet, as some of those I have talked to have asked, What is the *law?*

Are the police themselves under a duty to provide adequate safeguards against the secret, possibly unconstitutional questioning of suspects? Or shouldn't the legislatures, as many persons contend, address themselves to the problem and spell out in detail just how the police are to conduct such interrogations? More, shouldn't the legislatures decree under what precise circumstances a policeman may make an arrest and when he may not? Or when he may conduct a "reason-able" search and seizure, or may stop any citizen on the street for questioning in connection with any crime, or even to elicit information the policeman may need in carrying out his many other duties, such as enforcing traffic regulations and helping guard and protect the public safety?

Former New York City Police Commissioner Michael J. Murphy has said: "It's time the American people tell policemen how they want the law enforced, and back them to the hilt in doing it. We want and need legislative guidelines."

Absent such guidelines, various police departments, as already partially indicated, have endeavored to inaugurate practices which they believe will comply with the Supreme Court's guidelines. The New York City Police Department is now testing a program of tape-recorded interrogation. Said to be tamper-proof, the tape will run continuously for 24 hours a day, whether or not any questioning is actually going on. The New Orleans police, on the other hand, have installed a video-tape device which not only will record, but will show courts what happened during the questioning process.

Based partly on personal experience, this writer would favor the use of court stenographers or shorthand reporters in all police interrogations. Besides being able to record the questions and answers verbatim, the court reporter could also testify as to whether any subtle physical or psychological coercion went on.

Until definite guidelines are established for all local police forces throughout the country, the police will have to cope with the criminal element as best they can. Apprehension, arrest, and prosecution will have to be hit-and-miss affairs, subject in many cases to review and reversal by the Supreme Court of the United States.

Meanwhile, one question remains uppermost in the minds of all Americans, including policemen who know something about the real world outside the mahogany-paneled world of Supreme Court judges: While the court's absolutist doctrine coddles the criminals and cripples police departments, who is going to protect the innocent victim of crime, the rape victim made pregnant by the rapist, the man maimed by the mugger, the woman foully murdered in the street in full view of persons too afraid to come to the aid of another human being?

Perhaps the five men who sit in their pillared palace in Washington, D. C. will protect us. God help us, each and every one of us, if that kind of protection should be proffered. Give each of the five a badge, a club, and a gun; and I'll wager that once they forsake their law books and emerge into the world of reality, they'll be about as potent as jellyfish stranded on some sun-baked shore.

CHAPTER FOUR

What Price Crime?

AN ABRUPT LOOK of cold fright stole into the eyes of the mother who had just kissed her Washington, D. C.-bound teenage son and daughter goodbye. "Be careful where you go in Washington," she admonished them. "And whatever you do, don't go into any churches."

"Churches?" the son echoed as both youngsters eyed their mother quizzically. "What in the world have you suddenly got against churches?"

"Oh, nothing *against* churches," the mother answered hastily. "It's just that so many crimes have been committed in Washington churches lately. They're dangerous places to go into; that's all."

Were this mother's fears exaggerated, overmagnified, unfounded? Hardly. Crimes *inside* churches, those long reverently regarded sanctuaries against evils of all kinds, have been on the increase; and Washington, D. C. has pretty much led the nation in the amount of crimes against churchgoers accustomed to supplicating themselves before God in houses of worship.

Bear witness:

On a July afternoon several years ago a Congressman's secretary was stabbed in St. Peter's Church.

And on another day, just as ignominious a day as far as Washington, D. C. is concerned, the wife of a Southern Baptist minister visiting the nation's Capital with her husband was raped.

Purse-snatchings, muggings, looting, and harassment got so bad in Washington, in fact, that many churches had to inaugurate emergency precautions to protect their parishioners.

Old St. Joseph's Church on Capitol Hill canceled choir practice at night. "Walking on the streets," its notice said, was just too dangerous to permit nighttime choir rehearsal. And St. Joseph's, mind you, is a stone's throw from the New Senate Office Building and about three or four minutes' walk from the Supreme Court Building wherein sits the

30

court whose decisions are tying the hands of police and giving judicial blessings to criminals.

All Souls Memorial Church took another tack. It installed a ceiling-high gate to protect secretaries in the Parish Hall. And this sign was affixed to the door of the National City Christian Church: "For admittance, press button, and talk into the mike above when you get a response from the office."

Unbelievable? Read on.

Not only Washington's churches have taken precautions against the criminal element in the nation's Capital. The State Department posted extra guards in its main building to prevent attacks on women. Precautions like this one were necessary in the wake of reports that the wife of a State Department employee was raped by three men, that a secretary in the African Embassy was raped, and that an 18-year-old cleaning girl was raped in the women's room of the Agricultural Building, all within a span of a few weeks.

Washington, the nation's Capital, the seat of our Federal Government, can also lay claim to other, albeit somewhat dubious, distinctions. In 1962, for example, it led the nation's cities in the proportionate amount of murders and aggravated assaults committed within its precincts. Only Chicago with its storied history as an incubator of crime ran a fairly close second.

With Washington winning this kind of "acclaim" for crime within its borders, something happened to worsen the situation. "Investigative arrests" were forbidden in an effort to comply with pro-crime court decisions. An officer was denied leave to question or detain a suspect unless he arrested him, and that he could do only for "probable cause."

As an inevitable consequence, crime has blossomed better than cherry trees in the nation's Capital, and the hard-pressed police have been heard to complain that they have been forced by court decisions to change police procedures in such a way that they will result in "fewer solved crimes, and, eventually, more crimes in general."

Granted, the chronicle of crime in Washington could just as well be applied to dozens of other American cities. In almost any city in this nation there have been broad-daylight purse-snatchings, robberies, assaults on the streets, often in full view of other citizens too scared to do anything about the crimes being committed right before their eyes.

And in other cities, too, crime has occurred within the sacred portals of churches. Nor was it a case of some scoundrel simply pilfering the poor box. In College Point, a small community within New York City which might be called an intra-city suburb, so "uncitified" is it in appearance, a woman kneeling in prayer in a church was the victim of an attack for which she received hospital treatment.

And some months later, in early 1967, a 16-year-old Merrick, New York, girl was raped in the Cure of Ars Roman Catholic Church, also in Merrick. She had lit a candle and was kneeling in prayer beseeching God's protection for her brother fighting in Vietnam. As she rose from her knees, she was confronted by a stranger who leered at her and said, "Hello, baby." Frantic with fear, she ran up a side aisle toward the safety of the front doors, but the man ran down another aisle and caught her easily. She screamed and broke away momentarily, but he grabbed her again, this time around the throat, and hissed: "Don't make any noise or I'll kill you!" With that, he tossed her to the floor behind the last pews and raped her. A noise frightened the rapist off before he could visit further harm upon the terrified girl.

Armed with a description of the attacker provided by the victim of sexual assault in the house of God, the police picked up a suspect just three days later. The accused had been arrested once before and charged with robbery following an assault upon an 18-year-old girl who had been grabbed from behind in a Suffolk County, New York, church, rendered semi-unconscious, and partially disrobed before her screams scared her attacker off.

Surely, the epidemic of violence in our cities and in thousands of neighborhoods throughout the country has reached its untoppable peak when this kind of crime can happen in our houses of worship, long regarded as havens from evil in all its ugly forms.

Yet, it is at this point that Americans must ask themselves, Isn't anybody safe any more? Are we a nation of animals or a nation of men, women, and children governed by laws? And the simple answer to those questions is that while the criminal element in this country remains unchecked because of overlenient courts or the indifference of citizens, even the churches, those holy edifices of God, those "sanctuaries against all evil," are no longer safe for the prayerful, the worshipful, the penitent who would commune with God.

Crime, concededly, is godless. Its perpetrators know no god except lust, except greed, except the conscienceless will to injure or kill others or to seize their property.

Is it any wonder that the fear of violence which has gripped many

Americans and changed the patterns of their lives, not to say the life-patterns of some wearers of the cloth and their flocks, causes an anxious mother to warn her children *not* to dare enter any church in the nation's Capital?

As I see it, fear, the abstract emotion of fear, which, like a human life, has no dollars-and-cents value, is the appalling price we all must pay for crime in America. Fear, that devastator of one's peace of mind, keeps us from exchanging the ordinary pleasantries and amenities with one another. It keeps many of us from visiting public libraries at night, especially if shadowy streets have to be traversed to get there. It literally bars many women in particular from nighttime PTA or other meetings, and it denies countless thousands of us the use of our parks after dark.

More years ago than I care to remember I used to sit on a bench in New York City's world-famed Central Park with a young lady. Both of us were filled with the expectations of youth, and Central Park in those days was an ideal place in which to "exchange pleasantries" when the shades of night had enveloped it. But today, unless I were heavily armed for self-protection, I would no more think of sitting in Central Park at night than I would of jumping off the Brooklyn Bridge.

Stark fear, fear of personal violence at the hands of the felon, has other natural and logical byproducts: It makes man, the social animal, a good deal less sociable. It leads to withdrawal and mutual distrust. And when we hear that stealthy footstep behind us on a darkened street, we don't know whether to run, to yell for help, or to turn about prepared to do battle, tooth and nail, for our very survival.

As this kind of fear pervades and invades our lives, society itself suffers. The costs are incalculable, but they are nonetheless there. As a result, one gains the impression that society is both untrustworthy and unstable and that moral decay is being fostered by many forces, some of them governmental, which the ordinary citizen believes to be entirely beyond his control. Thus, as the crime rate climbs higher and higher, so does our distrust in the society that spawns it reach dizzying heights.

Other segments of our society, including some bodies rather formidable in stature, such as the President's Commission on Law Enforcement and Administration of Justice (immediately dubbed the "President's Crime Commission" by the mass media), have recognized the fact that crimes of violence strike fear into the hearts of many

Americans. But in its report titled, *The Challenge of Crime in a Free Society,** issued in February, 1967, the President's Crime Commission, though frankly admitting it could not tell Americans "how fearful they should be," nevertheless sought to underplay the statistical importance of crimes of violence and the fear that they generate. Our fears, the report implies, may be exaggerated because "publicity about total crime figures" does not distinguish between the "trends for property crime and those for crimes against persons," thereby creating "mistaken ideas about what is actually happening."

True, property crimes do occur more often than crimes of *personal* violence. Yet, what the President's Commission didn't seem to realize is that the American people regard human life as a good deal more precious than physical property. After all, what good is property if some criminal may see to it that you don't live to enjoy it?

On the other hand, the Commission didn't discount the price of fear in human values altogether. On the contrary, one of its own surveys, taken in high-crime districts in Boston and Chicago, showed that people responded to the high incidence of crime by changing the habits of their lives rather drastically. Forty-three percent reported they stayed completely off the streets at night. An additional 21 percent said they always used cars or taxis after dark. And 35 percent said they would no longer talk to strangers.

Figures like these are in and of themselves frightening. They show what fear, sometimes almost inexplicable, at times a bit unreasonable, can do to the human spirit.

Verily, it can keep us out of our churches. And that fact alone is the one weighty indictment of the criminal element and pro-criminal element in America. For if we cannot live like normal human beings in this "land of the free," free to walk the streets at any time and free to follow our normal pursuits in our quest for happiness and contentment in this world—and, yes, free to worship God as we choose—without fear for our lives and the lives of our loved ones, then this land of the free and home of the brave has become the land of the fettered and the home of the terrorized. Maybe it is only abject fear that shackles us and blights our lives, but it might just as well be leg irons.

There are ways by which we can banish fear of personal violence at the hands of criminals from our minds and hearts. Those will be discussed in the final chapter. Suffice to say that fear, stark, unreason-

---

* Obtainable at $2.25 each from Supt. of Documents, U. S. Government Printing Office, Washington, D. C. 20402.

ing, sometimes unbridled fear governs all of us to a degree as we ponder the problem of crime in the United States.

Let us refer now to the staggering economic costs of crime, and the number of crimes committed in a given year.

One report I read states that known crime costs Americans $15 billion a year. My own figure, culled from several sources, is that the estimated cost per year is more like $21 billion. And that, mind you, is the estimated cost of known crimes in America, crimes actually reported to police sources. The President's Crime Commission says actual crime is several times the reported figure. If that be so, and there is no reason to doubt it, then the actual cost of crime, if not two-or three-fold higher than the $21 billion figure, tops that figure by at least several billions of dollars.

While there have been a few leveling off or fairly static periods in between time, crime has generally climbed since 1933. At that time your chances of having your property stolen were one out of 320. Today they are one out of 166, or about twice as likely. Again, the chance of personal attack in 1933 was one out of 700. Today is is one out of 550.

Geography can make a difference. By and large, Americans can feel relatively safer in the country or the suburbs since most serious crimes occur in the cities. To underscore the point, 26 cities with only 18 percent of the population have a third of all the crime.

In the last ten years, crime has risen steadily in the United States; and in the last five years, it has jumped 33 percent.

To cite crime totals for a representative year, 1965 (the latest figures available from the FBI's Uniform Crime Reports, also heavily relied upon by the President's Crime Commission), in that year there were 3,665,860 offenses reported to the police. (Let us re-emphasize that the Crime Commission says actual unreported crime is *several times* the reported figure.)

This 3,666,000 figure represents a jump of 22.3 percent over the average number of 2,997,815 offenses committed during the 1960-64 period.

Murder merits special mention. There were 6,934 murders or non-negligent manslaughters during 1965. This compares with 5,828 similar crimes, on an average, during the 1960-64 period.

Forcible rapes showed by far the greatest hike, 31.5 percent, or a total of 16,554 in 1965 as against the 1960-64 average of 12,592.

If other serious crimes have not exactly skyrocketed, they nevertheless have shown substantial increases. Aggravated assaults were up to 136,644 in 1965 compared to the 107,790 average during 1960-64.

And so the list goes: Burglary or breaking and entering escalated to a 919,203 figure, as compared with an average of 734,205 in 1960-64. And larcenies of $50 or over rocketed to 603,366 in 1965, as against an average of 460,861 in 1960-64.

The ever-mounting crimes committed by the "restless" youth of our land were perhaps best reflected in the amount of auto thefts, the prime "crime of the young," which zoomed to 417,795 in 1965 as compared with an average of 321,790 in the 1960-64 period.

The FBI Reports note that the "total number of criminal acts that occur is unknown," but it does its best to get all police departments to report all crimes that come to their attention.

I could cite facts and figures ad nauseam, but the recitation would serve little purpose beyond showing that crime is climbing at a rate so alarming that the American people must act and act quickly to curb criminality in the United States.

One further statistic does merit mention, though. In 1963 the FBI initiated a study of the criminal careers of 134,938 individual offenders, mostly Federal offenders whose crimes were "also of a local nature." Of the 135,000 offenders processed, three out of four were shown to be repeaters—"recidivists" is the fancy word used by some law enforcement officials, criminologists, and others. Just think of it: Seventy-five percent had on their record at least one prior arrest on some charge. The entire sampling had an average criminal career of more than ten years, during which they averaged five arrests, 2.4 convictions, and 1.5 imprisonments.

And now this is the salient point: "Leniency in the form of probation, suspended sentences, parole, and conditional release had been afforded 51 percent of the offenders." After the first leniency, the group averaged more than three new arrests.

Just as significantly, the 1965 Reports states that since 1962 acquittals and dismissals for serious crimes as a group (murder, aggravated assault, rape, etc.) had risen 14 percent.

Since Miranda, the figure is undoubtedly higher. In February, 1967, for instance, Brooklyn, New York, District Attorney Aaron Koota disclosed that since the Miranda decision in June, 1966, ten defendants charged with murder, rape, robbery, and kidnapping had been set free. To further illustrate the impact of the U. S. Supreme Court's criminal-pampering decision, Mr. Koota revealed that of 316 persons arrested for major crimes from June to September, 1966, 130 refused to make any statement at all after having been advised of their rights.

"The court has weighted the scales of justice heavily in favor of the criminal suspect, to the detriment of the decent, law-abiding citizens of our community," Mr. Koota observed.

The scales of justice are indeed now weighted in favor of the criminal, and fear for personal safety has largely vanquished reason in this land. Unless positive, vigorous steps are taken to turn fear into constructive action aimed at targeting in on the criminal element and the kind of thinking that makes crime profitable and so often unpunishable, then those who would like to see the ownership of guns seriously restricted may live to see America an armed camp, whether guns and other weapons are licit or illicit. In that event, each American will become his own police officer prepared to protect himself. Each will reason that there is no other way since the courts of this country have more compassion for the criminal than they do for his victim.

Whether Americans who think like that are right or wrong, the will to survive runs strong in all of us. But if lex talionis—the law of retaliation—comes into play, if each law-abiding American takes up arms and becomes his own policeman simply because there is no other recourse, then and only then will this nation understand the awful, the ultimate price of fear.

The self-arming of the citizenry need not come to pass, of course. It will not if we act quickly and wisely and with a resolve that will permit all Americans to walk the streets of this land—or even to enter churches—at any time, day or night, without fear of being murdered or physically assaulted.*

---

* Although the FBI Uniform Crime Reports for 1966 were not available as this book went to the printer, the press reported that the 1966 Reports show that the volume of crime in the U. S. has rocketed 62 percent since 1960, while national growth was a mere 9 percent. The Reports further indicate that violent crimes jumped 11 percent during 1966 alone and that the number of crimes rose 11.4 percent over 1965. At the same time, the number of serious crimes solved was only 24 percent, a drop of 8 percent below the number solved during 1965, and a drop of 8 percent below the average for the previous five-year period. Also, during 1966 there were 3.25 million serious crimes committed, including an estimated 10,920 homicides.

During the first six months of 1967 the crime rate continued to soar spectacularly, rising another 18 percent over the first six months in 1966, according to reports.

The drop in the number of crimes solved may in part be attributable to the interference of the courts in police investigative procedures.

CHAPTER FIVE

The President's Crime Commission

IN ITS 340-page paper-covered book, *The Challenge of Crime in a Free Society,* the President's Crime Commission advances over 200 recommendations aimed mainly at reducing crime in America. While I may touch upon many of these recommendations, since the major emphasis of this particular book is on the police power—or lack of it—I shall pretty much hew to that specific subject.

Perhaps the most significant recommendation of the Commission in that regard is that three kinds of policeman be established throughout the United States: the community service officer (CSO), the police officer, and the police agent.

The police agent would be a man of "considerable educational attainment"—at least two years of college and preferably with a baccalaureate degree in the liberal arts or social sciences (a strange, though euphemistic, term descriptive of something that doesn't actually exist).

Despite the educational requirements, the Commission would open the door to police-agent status to officers who had "shown their capacity for imaginative and responsible police work." Perhaps in a way the Commission thus admits, however grudgingly, that talent will out no matter what a man's education.

The police agent would do "complicated, sensitive, and demanding" police jobs. He might be a juvenile officer, a community relations officer, a career specialist in narcotics or in robbery or homicide investigations. Or, on the other hand, he might be a uniformed officer patrolling streets in high-crime neighborhoods.

At any rate, as the Commission sees it, the agent would be the "most knowledgeable and responsible member of the police team." He would also be an innovator, devising new techniques and procedures—but not without the official sanction of the U. S. Supreme Court, I would assume.

The regular police officer would be pretty much what he is today. He would enforce the laws and conduct immediate follow-up investigations to uncover suspects close to the scene of crime. He would perform routine patrol, respond to emergencies, enforce traffic regulations, and investigate traffic accidents. He would work in concert with police agents and community service officers.

The community service officer, a self-explanatory term, would be of a slightly different breed. Typically young, from 17 to 21 years old, with the aptitude, integrity, and stability needed for sensitive police work, he would be a kind of apprentice policeman "replacing the present cadet." His work would be closely supervised by the police agent and police officer. He would not have full law enforcement powers or carry arms, nor would he perform any clerical duties. Somewhat similar to a presentday member of a police youth squad, he would maintain close contact with juveniles.

A community service officer might be accepted as such even though he had a minor offense record. The Commission points out that otherwise it could conceivably be very difficult to recruit members from minority groups as it is "more likely than not that a Negro youth who grows up in a slum will have such a record." The CSO would continue his studies at the expense of the department and would be expected to qualify as a police agent or officer as soon as possible.

Pointing out that about two-thirds of the police departments in medium-sized and big cities are below their authorized police strength, the Commission called for more active recruitment, especially on college campuses and in "inner-city neighborhoods."

It took no notice of the fact that recruitment may be partly complicated by such things as morale (who wants to be the scapegoat in a social revolution, for example?) and low pay, although it did recommend that pay scales be drastically revised upward. Suggesting a re-examination of police salary scales, it cites the relatively low median annual pay for policemen in small cities, a mere $4,600. In large cities it is only $5,300. And typically, the report says, "the maximum salary for nearly all positions is less than $1,000 over the starting salary." Recruitment problems? Why not?

(One wonders whether teachers who constantly clamor for more pay, more pay, would put their lives on the line for that kind of money.)

A special agent of the Federal Bureau of Investigation gets an initial salary of $8,421 a year. If he serves long enough and ably enough, he can pull down a salary of $16,905, and that without being promoted to a supervisory position.

The Commission concedes that a police salary scale such as the FBI's is out of the question, particularly in smaller cities and villages. However, it recommends the FBI scale as a standard against which all cities should measure their own "potential for attracting able recruits."

The Commission claims that at least some of our big cities should be able to match the FBI's starting rate of pay ($8,421) immediately or within the near future, at least for the police agent position. It suggests that a police officer's salary might be $1,000 a year less than that of the agent, while the salary of the community service officer, the apprentice policeman, should be about $5,000 a year.

To take New York City, which has a police force of 28,000, for comparison purposes, a rookie patrolman got a starting salary as of July 1, 1966, of $7,032. As a result of negotiations with the city during early 1967, according to a police source, the new appointee could, in three years, reach a salary of $9,383, the top minimum salary of a first-grade patrolman. So it can be seen that while the rookie's starting salary might be described as low, he can advance, after a minimum of three years' service, to a fairly respectable salary which compares favorably with the beginning salary of an FBI agent.

Actually, there is almost nothing new in the Commission's recommendations treated with so far. More than 70 percent of police departments throughout the country require at least a high school diploma now. Many big cities have police academies in which recruits are trained. Again using New York City as an example, it requires new patrolmen to take a training course for four months at its police academy. During that interval, the recruit earns 10 college credits which may be applied to a police science degree at City College. The department has in that way acquired hundreds of college graduates, and the educational effort is continuing.

Changing terms doesn't necessarily change functions. The police agent may be likened to the present-day detective, although the detective may, initially at any rate, be the superior of the agent because, if he has come up through the ranks, he will undoubtedly boast a wealth of on-the-job experience and training rather than just a college education in untested and untried theories.

The idea of a community service officer is not new at all. Many departments have his equivalent on youth squads, men who have daily contact with juveniles in troubled areas. Like the CSO presumably would, they attempt to lead the juvenile away from the crooked road of the criminal and into the straight-and-narrow path of the productive, law-abiding citizen.

The Commission's recommendation that the CSO not carry arms is unsound. In that event, the apprentice officer might see a crime—a serious crime like murder—committed before his own eyes and be powerless to do anything about it beyond possibly attempting to summon help. In the meantime, the criminal could easily escape or even kill the CSO if he attempted to interfere in the slightest way.

The Commission has also called for recruitment of minority-group officers in communities with substantial minority populations. Here again, many departments have actually done this already. Negroes and whites often work side by side in minority neighborhoods. For all that, no one can gainsay that this recommendation is a good one. A man who understands the members of his own racial or ethnic group is naturally able to deal with them, generally speaking, in a more efficient fashion than could a non-member of the particular group or race.

If a Negro policeman, for example, arrests another Negro in a minority-group neighborhood, the charge of "police brutality" is less likely to be hurled at him than would be so in the case of the white policeman arresting the Negro.

The President's Crime Commission has additionally recommended citizens advisory groups in police precincts with large minority populations. That too has already come to pass in at least some cities. Quite understandably, such groups are desirable to promote understanding and a mutuality of trust as between the neighborhood and the policeman who must endeavor to preserve law and order in that neighborhood.

I would go so far as to recommend that police departments, at least the larger ones, set up police speakers bureaus whose members would, on invitation, address PTA and other community service groups and address high school and even grammar school students, etc., explaining the functions of the police and the need for community cooperation and help if the policeman is to do his work effectively.

No one should have illusions about this type of program in high-crime neighborhoods that are not too responsive to the "public relations" appeal. In those areas a strong police contingent should be on hand to act as a direct deterrent to crime as far as possible.

"The heart of the police law enforcement effort is patrol, the movement around an assigned area, on foot or by vehicle, of uniformed policemen." So says the Crime Commission report.

The policeman on patrol is perhaps the greatest single deterrent to street crime simply because of his physical presence. Just as putting a police officer on every New York City subway train during the late night hours reduced subway crime in that city by 36 percent in 1966, so, too, does regular, periodic movement cut offenses in high-crime areas when patrols are beefed up.

In that connection, shouldn't the auxiliary police, those unpaid and unsung volunteers who stand ready and willing to do a job, be put to good use in low-crime sections initially and in high-crime areas eventually?

In a letter to the editor of the Long Island, New York, PRESS, Graham Mark Schneider, President of the Auxiliary Police Benevolent Association in Manhattan, recommended giving "some type of peace officer status" to auxiliary policemen. He said:

"Many of our streets are not safe to walk on during the evening. The streets could adequately be patrolled with more Auxiliary Police. Thousands of men refuse to join and many thousands have left because the Auxiliary Police have no authority other than to make a citizen's arrest in the event one is needed.

"If some type of peace officer status were given to them, at least 10,000 men could be put on the streets. These men could assist the regular patrolmen and certainly reduce the rate of crime.

"If the people of the various communities are genuinely concerned about the rising tide of crime, let them write their councilmen and assemblymen and tell them to give the Auxiliary Police authority to do an effective job."

The 10,000 men Mr. Schneider referred to would presumably augment New York City's 28,000 regular police officers and could assuredly render splendid assistance on foot patrol especially. Why not accept this generous offer of help from citizens so concerned that they are ready to endanger their own lives to be of assistance? All big cities who have these Auxiliary Policemen might well think about expanding their effectiveness through broader use.

Whether these volunteer policemen should be permitted to carry arms should be left up to particular departments or perhaps to state legislatures. In any event, all officers, whether regulars or auxiliaries, should be proved to be skillful in the handling of various weapons before being allowed to carry them.

The Commission made many other recommendations about the police, including the employment of lawyers as legal advisors. With court decisions hobbling law enforcement, the patrolman today almost needs a lawyer at his elbow before deciding whether to arrest anyone he may catch in the act of committing a crime. In fact, one critic I know said sourly: "No policeman should arrest anybody until he gets the U. S. Supreme Court on the phone and asks for advance advice on whether the arrest will stick or not."

More than anything else, this kind of acidulous criticism indicates a loss of confidence not in the police, but in the courts of the land. On page 81 of its report, the President's Crime Commission says: "The juvenile court is a court of law, charged like other agencies of criminal justice with protecting the community against threatening conduct." That statement says a mouthful. If the juvenile courts are charged with "protecting the community against threatening conduct," shouldn't the U. S. Supreme Court be under a similar duty to protect the nation against threatening conduct? Just how it protects society by permitting criminals to literally get away with murder is not readily discernible.

Although the 200-plus recommendations of the President's Crime Commission are meant to strengthen and improve law enforcement in America, hence protecting the potential victim of crime, no direct recommendation is made on how the victim may protect himself. The Commission does say, though, that "public concern about crime . . . can be a powerful force of action." Then it goes on to lament the failure of the public to take very much interest in crime. The public, it explains, considers crime largely a matter for the police, the courts, and other public agencies.

The report deals at some length with what can be done ex post facto to help the victims of crime. It enunciates a proposal often heard these days that crime victims be publicly compensated for physical injuries from violent crimes. California, the Commission points out, was the first state to compensate the crime victim with limited financial resources; and its program is continuing. New York State has a similar law, making compensation awards only to crime victims suffering "serious financial hardship."

No doubt, some kind of crime insurance setup should be provided in every state for the victim of crime who is at least partially so victimized because the state itself if powerless to protect him. Why not tap all gambling receipts to help pay for crime insurance? Since gambling is a crime in one place in this country and not a crime in another, especially if conducted under government auspicies (such are the double, triple, quadruple standards of some of our governments), a portion of the "criminal, non-criminal" proceeds of gambling could well be set aside to aid the victims of crime.

There are other ways, concededly, in which the crime victim could be compensated. Says the Crime Commission report: ". . . the criminal law generally makes no effort to use its sanctions to insure restitution to the victim. Indeed, it often aggravates the victim's problem by incarcerating the offender, thus preventing him from earning money to make restitution."

That state of affairs could be easily remedied if judges were empowered, when putting a convict on probation, to order the man to work and make restitution over a number of weeks or even years, if need be, to his victim. Parole boards releasing a man from prison could perform a similar function.

Victims of crime and potential victims of crime, faced with their society's failure to keep criminality in check in America, are increasingly doing for themselves what their society is unable to do for them. The sale of guns is actually spiraling upward in some areas, for example, despite the anti-gun ownership drive now in full swing in this country. More about this subject in Chapter 8, "Ways to Combat Crime."

One of the more persuasive recommendations of the Commission is that concerning the pooling of police resources. Pointing again to California, where more than 500 intergovernmental agreements exist under which one jurisdiction contracts with another for some or all of its police services, it calls for the consolidation of police services by counties and metropolitan areas to "provide the most satisfactory law enforcement service and protection at the lowest possible cost."

The value of this suggestion is self-apparent. But why not go a lot further? Since early youth, I have entertained the notion that organized crime in its present octopusean form simply could not exist if all police departments in the country, including the Federal Bureau of Investigation, were united in a total, all-out war against syndicated criminality. Legislation by the Congress and the respective states would probably be needed to implement such a crime-stopping scheme, but that obstacle certainly is not insurmountable. Special task forces, including Federal, state, and local police experts, could be set up to uncover and systematically eradicate particular kinds of crime. If there were some objections to the intervention of the Federal Government in local situations which did not involve crimes of an essentially Federal or interstate nature, those objections could likely be overcome by legislating to permit state and local forces to invite the FBI to help out in a given battle against local crime.

Many fire departments, even those of the strictly volunteer type, have agreements permitting them to cooperate with departments outside their specific area of protection. Why can't police not only do that on a local basis, but on a state and national basis as well? They, of course, can if whatever legislation is required is speedily enacted.

There is, admittedly, always some danger in allowing the Federal Government to assume control of any function essentially local in nature; and that would include the local police function.

On March 27, 1967, the Associated Press quoted Congressman Richard H. Poff (R-Va.), chairman of a newly organized task force on crime, as praising the Commission's crime report in general, but disagreeing with some details. His main fear, the story said, is a "mammoth police pyramid with its apex centered in Washington and its base spread into every precinct and hamlet in America."

The danger of centralized government gargantuan in form and power such as is the Federal Government which now practically predetermines how every law-abiding citizen (note that I except the criminal element) shall live and breathe in this country is ever present. That's precisely why the Federal Government, even in a national drive against crime, should become the partner, not the master, of the state and local police and only come into the picture at all on invitation of the respective states.

We should not, though, in our zeal to keep the Federal Government from becoming the complete dictator of life in America, allow a division of police power and a fragmentation of effort to stand in the way of the ultimate defeat of organized crime in America. Or in the way of the cutting of the crime rate in general.

Other strident voices critical of the President's Crime Commission report have been heard. Congressman John W. Wydler (R-N.Y.) has said the report wrongly emphasizes a long-range strategy of social improvement to offset crime rather than direct crime-control measures. He too complained that public safety is jeopardized by "handcuffed police," timid judges, and legal decisions which protect violent criminals. In an oblique reference to the Miranda decision, he proposed the passing of "no nonsense" laws to give police reasonable powers to take confessions.

And during the middle of February, 1967, the St. Paul, Minnesota, PIONEER PRESS made a survey of the reactions of local law enforcement officials to the Crime Commission report. It quoted St. Paul Police Chief Lester E. McAuliffe as noting that money alone is not the answer to the problem of crime. He doubted, as do many other critics of the Crime Commission report, that the Commission's efforts will do much to protect *now*, when the crime rate is climbing steadily.

Chief McAuliffe topped off his criticism by citing facts and figures relative to crime in his own city. Major crimes, said he, declined 3.8 percent in 1965; but as a result of U. S. Supreme Court decisions broadening the rights of the accused, the major-crime rate just about doubled in 1966, hitting a 7.5 percentage.

Like his counterpart in St. Paul, the police chief of Minneapolis was not exactly enthusiastic about the Commission's report. He likewise emphasized the immediacy of the crime problem. "We need help right now to protect our Minneapolis citizens," he said. He echoed the sentiments of many policemen who say more manpower and equipment is needed now, not in the near or distant future, if the police are to crack down on crime before it gets completely out of hand.

While conceding that some of the Commission's long-range plans may have a beneficial effect in time, the Minneapolis police chief said simply: "I'm worried about today and tomorrow."

That forms of crime can get completely out of hand was amply demonstrated by a rather spectacular picture which appeared in the New York DAILY NEWS during the Cleveland riots in 1966. It showed a looter emerging from a store with a fan or some other appliance in his hands while a policeman stood by powerless to act.

The PIONEER PRESS quoted St. Paul Deputy Chief of Police for Detectives Richard H. Rowan as scoring the Commission's findings as the "same answers such groups always come up with when they are preoccupied with sociological questions."

Like some of his colleagues, he stressed the need for more police and a get-tough approach to crime. Nor did he admit that social factors are the primary causes of crime. In fact, he cast doubt on the widely held belief that poverty alone can explain the skyrocketing crime rate.

As many critics of the Commission report contend, money itself is never the complete cure for anything, including crime (any more than it is the cure for a dread disease like cancer, still the scourge of mankind despite the millions that have been poured into the war against that killer).

Mr. Rowan also took exception to recent court decisions which protect the criminal rather than his victim. Said he: "The courts seem determined to protect the offender by putting legal handcuffs on the police instead of on the rapist, killer, and robber."

To try to be objective about a matter that is really more subjective than objective in its very essence and nature, the Commission's report, despite its deficiencies, has at least this value: It is a start, a beginning. It offers no panaceas, no cure-alls, because for the vicious disease of crime, which can, like cancer, metastasize or spread with death-dealing and morale-killing rapidity, there just isn't any simple answer, any sure cure-all.

In its report the Commission has many answers for a very complex problem. But it did suggest one answer which I consider to be the most compelling, the most forceful, the most likely to achieve lasting, long-range results. It cited a 1965 Gallup poll which asked people what they thought responsible for the increase in crime. Strangely, but not too strangely at that, the polltakers found that the bulk of the reasons advanced had to do directly with the *moral character of the population* rather than with changes in objective circumstances or with law enforcement. Other responses stressed "poor parental guidance," people expecting "too much," and people wanting "something for nothing." Indeed, only a few of the answers gave objective conditions such as the automobile, the population explosion, or poverty or unemployment as causes of crime.

"Public concern about crime is mounting," says the report. Certainly it is. And the situation is going to get a lot worse before it gets better if the constantly rising crime rate during the last decade or so has any meaning at all.

The public concern, however, shouldn't reflect itself in mere lip service to worry. We the people should sit ourselves down and write letters to our respective legislators, local, state, and national, demanding a nationwide drive against crime and its causes. If syndicated and other hideous forms of crime threaten the lives or well-being of us all, let us bring all the forces of our society to bear on the problem and wipe it out, much as a skilled surgeon would excise a cancer. If the moral climate in which they are reared poisons the minds of our children, let us drastically change that moral climate.

But first and foremost, let us support our police, local, state, and national. If they are our first line of defense against the criminal, they are in many situations our only line of defense.

Catherine Genovese might not have died ignominiously as dawn was breaking on a New York City street if some of the 38 persons who admitted having heard her cries for help as she was being stabbed repeatedly had gone to her aid. Or she might be alive and well today if any of the 38 persons who could hear, if not see, the evidence of a foul murder being committed on the street had promptly called the police. It takes rare, raw courage to face a knife-wielding murderer. But it takes no courage and very little effort to lift a telephone from its receiver and summon the police.

It does take courage to offer the helping hand that may save a life. But that's the kind of courage that's needed from the public itself if the cancerous death-dealer called crime is to be driven out of our hearts, out of our homes, and out of our land. Let us remember and let all who like to talk about our freedoms remember that in this country we are free to live as law-abiding citizens, not as criminals bent on destroying all that is good and decent.

Let us remember and at the same time never allow the criminal to forget the meaning of freedom in America.

CHAPTER SIX

Civilian Review Boards

"IN GOING BEYOND the established legal procedures, the (President's Crime) Commission finds it unreasonable to single out the police as the only agency that should be subject to special scrutiny from the outside. The Commission therefore *does not* recommend the establishment of civilian review boards in jurisdictions where they do not exist, solely to review police conduct." (Emphasis supplied.)

This statement by the Crime Commission is remarkable and startling on two counts: (1) because so many politicians and other public figures have in the past outspokenly advocated civilian-dominated police review boards; and (2) because President Lyndon B. Johnson, who established the Crime Commission, has been closely identified with and a strong supporter of the civil rights movement, whose leaders have used the police as prime targets.

The reason the Commission gives for its unexpected anti-review board position is absorbing, to say the least. It says: "The police are only one of a number of official agencies with whom the public has contact, and in some cases, because they are the most visible and conspicuous representatives of local government, they may be the focus of more attention than they deserve. Incompetence and mistreatment by housing, sanitation, health, and welfare officials can be as injurious to citizens as mistreatment by the police and should be equally subject to public scrutiny. These officials, like policemen, are public servants. In view of the increasing involvement of government officials in the lives of citizens, adequate procedures for the consideration of such individual grievances as citizens may have against such officials are essential to effective government. So far as possible, it is desirable that such procedures be established within the governmental agency involved. To the extent such procedures are ineffective or fail to inspire general public confidence of those who may have legitimate grievances, further recourse is essential. The form that such further recourse should take is dependent on local needs and governmental structure."

The Commission follows up its candid opinion of the lack of necessity for civilian-dominated police review boards with this sweeping recommendation:

"Every jurisdiction should provide adequate procedures for full and fair processing of all citizen grievances and complaints about the conduct of any public officer or employee."

The growing popularity in the United States of the ombudsman, an impartial citizen presumably above and beyond the reach of politics and politicians, to listen to citizens' grievances and right wrongs committed by public employees or officials wherever possible is, in and of itself, a tacit admission that policemen are not the only public servants whose actions in given situations might well be subjected to public scrutiny.

But, taking the Commission's wide-ranging recommendation at face value, it would likely mean that every agency of government, large or small, would have within it something equivalent to a complaint bureau or review board to which citizens could appeal for redress of grievances against employees or officials of that particular agency.

Thus, one can conceive complaint bureaus set up to hear citizen grievances in the following branches of government, among others, or within the following groups which in one way or the other seek—or should seek—the approbation of the public:

1. Welfare departments.

(Grievances could very well include citizens' complaints about the way welfare departments dole out the public's money to support employables who not only are capable of standing on their own two feet, but may be perfectly ready and willing to do so if given half a chance. Or about the manner in which welfare departments openly support promiscuity by not demanding legislative authority to seek out and haul unwed fathers into court and force them, by court order, to support the children they help bring into the world.)

2. Politicians of all stripes, whether public or mere political office holders.

(Here I fear we would need a complaint bureau or review board comprised of citizens interested not in politics, but in good, clean, honest government. Such bureaus or boards could call upon politicians, including elected officials, to publish the exact amounts and kinds of patronage they dispense in any given year. The figures should disclose how many job payoffs were made to faithful followers, relatives, or friends; how much in dollars and cents the political-plum handouts cost the taxpayers each year; how much this kind of subtle vote-buying with the people's own money hikes the tax rate; and other similarly embarrassing questions.

(Inquiries like these might spoil the spoils system operations of politicos a trifle, but there is no doubt they would be mighty edifying. Moreover, a public informed along these lines might vote a lot more intelligently during local, state, and national elections.)

3. Teachers.

(There could be teacher review boards or complaint bureaus with which parents could register complaints without fear of seeing their children become victims of reprisal. Complaints might include the objections of citizens to the way many teachers have thumbed their educated noses at the law by conducting strikes expressly prohibited by law and to the manner in which so many teachers have and are making unprofessional public spectacles of themselves.

(I can think of many other possible grievances against teachers, but since this book has to do with law and order primarily, this one sample will suffice for now.)

All sorts of review boards or grievance bureaus to inquire into the activities of professional people who become the objects of public complaint come to mind. Why not review boards for doctors, for dentists, for lawyers, for all sorts of white-collar men and women who, in carrying out their professional duties, have intimate contact with the public and must necessarily create a favorable public image?

Concededly, many professional groups have their own disciplinary boards now. Bar associations, for instance, have grievance committees to which citizens who believe a certain lawyer has "done them in" can appeal. The medical profession too has grievance boards to hear complaints against doctors.

Yet, since one of the chief objections to police interrogation of suspects is that the questioning is done in secret and is in effect a "secret trial," the same type of objection could be registered against many of the boards which ostensibly discipline the members of their own profession. Lawyers' grievance committee hearings generally are secret, and the public, which may have a strong interest in the activities of an attorney whose actions are questionable, is barred from such hearings.

The courts too are party to this "behind-closed-door" approach to disciplining members of the legal profession. One case I stenographically reported many years ago makes the point adequately. At the outset of the hearing, the judge cautioned everybody present not to divulge anything that went on in the locked courtroom. As I was a reporter for a local newspaper at the time, I was certain that his honor's remarks were directed mainly at me. The importance of the judge's admonition became forcefully apparent as a parade of bankers and other respected businessmen of the particular community took the stand as character witnesses in behalf of the attorney and praised to the heavens a man who had pleaded guilty to a serious crime. As I recorded the accolades of these pillars of their community, I began to wonder whether they would be quite so unstinting in their praise if their testimony had been given at a public hearing. I also wondered whether the public interest was truly being served by holding this type of hearing behind closed doors. I'm still wondering.

Mind you, in suggesting that complaint bureaus or review boards might be set up for people whose professions and educational attainments may make them peculiarly capable of taking unfair advantage of the public at large, I do not mean to imply by any means that I favor a superfluity of review boards. On the contrary, I think all agencies of government and people whose callings make them responsive to the people should be self-policing.

But hearings on complaints of the public against "governmenters" and members of professions should by all means be public so that the public's right to know just why kind of unethical conduct such persons are accused of is preserved.

Many of the professions claim they are self-policing now or that there are ways in which they can be "policed" such as by the preferring of criminal charges where indicated. That is true, but unethical conduct that does not involve criminal charges is rarely the subject of judicial review *in public,* and non-public hearings suggest that too many skeletons can be buried in too many closets.

Actually, most police departments have self-policing machinery that is far superior, generally speaking, to any that exists among other government agencies or among the various professions.

To begin with, police organizations are semi-military in nature. They are distinctive bodies which operate 24 hours a day. And in many areas, although eight-hour shifts are worked, the police are considered to be technically on duty 24 hours a day, subject to call during any of their off hours.

When faced with the necessity of making a split-second decision, they cannot, as doctors or lawyers might, go into consultation with other members of their calling. As a matter of fact, one of the very valid complaints of the police is that courts may sit in judgment for months before deciding whether the decision of a policeman made in a fraction of a second or perhaps in several seconds was right or wrong. In that connection, one wonders whether a judge or group of jurists which takes eight indecisive months to decide the rightness or wrongness of a policeman's conduct would ever qualify to wear the uniform of a policeman.

In any event, nothing raises the hackles of the average policeman more than the mere mention of a civilian review board of non-policemen armed with authority to question the conduct of the officer who, by education, training, and experience, considers himself qualified to do his job.

But why the focus on the policeman? Why not put the spotlight on the politician who gets his clutches on the people's money in deviously subtle ways? Or on the teacher whose own form of lawlessness and exhibitionism sets so fine an example for children? Or on college professors who give aid and comfort to the enemy by publicly proclaiming the hope that the Communists defeat us in the Vietnam war? Or on the lunacy of the professor or other "professional" who praises and recommends the use of drugs?

Why is the policeman the goat in the civil rights movement? Why not the Congress and the legislatures of the respective states, for certainly they have much more to do with civil rights or the lack of such rights than does the policeman?

There are many answers to the question as to why the policeman, not the legislator, is the direct target in the civil rights movement. The police are more directly in the public eye. They roam the streets. They have nose-to-nose and eye-to-eye contact with the public as they try to put down crime, especially in high-crime areas which are also coincidentally ghettos. There is almost an instinctive dislike for authority among many people, even though that authority is intended for their protection and to preserve the peace of a community.

Last but not least, because he is so much in the public eye, the policeman has become the symbol of a society against which other segments of society are now revolting. (Some, in fact, seem incapable of realizing just how revolting they are.) The policeman has therefore unwittingly become the scapegoat in an internecine war which he did not himself cause and over which he has little or no control.

As former New York City Police Commissioner Michael J. Murphy has observed: The work of the policeman is "no longer a matter of cops and robbers alone. It has become more a question of people and police, and the police have found themselves drawn into many problems, many grievances, for which they are not responsible and which they, as police, cannot solve."

Let us set to rest the oft-heard charge that the Communists are the actual ringleaders of the anti-police drive in America. They're not, although they do play a very active part in the "down-with-the-police" campaign. Anyone who believes otherwise is just too naive for words, for the evidence to the contrary is too strong for anyone to doubt.

It is too bad that the Federal Bureau of Investigation or the U. S. Attorney General doesn't release from time to time the names and addresses of known Communists all over the country so that we who stand foursquare for the preservation of our Republic, its freedoms, and ideals might know just who our enemies are. But the United States is, in a sense, a schizophrenic country. While our men—many of them only boys—are being killed by Communists in Vietnam, we pamper Communists within our own border because the Federal Constitution says we must tolerate the very persons who would, if given half a chance, rip that Constitution to shreds.

At any rate, J. Edgar Hoover, Director of the Federal Bureau of Investigation, has indicated that Communists are very directly and actively involved in the anti-police war. Said he in *U. S. News and World Report* on September 27, 1965:

"Not only do the Communists directly exploit unrest, but they frequently spread their germs of subversion through front groups and dupes. This tactic has become increasingly evident in recent demonstrations by young people where police have been charged with brutality in handling picket lines or demonstrations involving racial matters or protests against United States involvement in Vietnam.

"Communist adherents are schooled in methods of intimidating law enforcement. Whenever they are confronted by a law-enforcement officer, the word brutality is foremost upon their lips. It is their aim to humiliate, exasperate and provoke the law-enforcement officer in an effort to prevent his judicious and calm enforcement of the laws he is to uphold."

Hoover went on to say that he was not implying that "all charges of police brutality emanate from the Communists or their dupes." The charges, he said, were also coming from "many well-meaning, if ill-informed and poorly advised, citizens."

If one needed any further proof of the insidious influence of Communists on the young, he need only consider the professional "student," the 40-year-old Communist attending a college or university not for the purposes of learning, but simply to proselytize or convert suggestible American youths into confirmed and easily manipulated Communists.

This state of things is, again, a tribute to the toleration of Americans beyond the realm of reason and the bounds of self-interest and self-preservation.

But what about the charges of police brutality made not by Communists, but by sincere Americans who honestly believe the policeman is pretty much a beast capable of beating the average American with a rubber hose at the flick of an eyelash?

In the last few years anguished cries of "police brutality" have come from demonstrators enlisted in all sorts of causes—first and foremost, civil rights; secondly, the demand that the United States withdraw from Vietnam; and thirdly, the free-speech movement on college campuses.

Anyone who probes, in depth, the anti-police drive in America is certain to reach one conclusion: "Police brutality" is a false charge raised by people who want what they may consider the ultimate freedom: the freedom to break the law as they choose without the restraints that society normally imposes on lawbreakers.

There is no convincing evidence of any wave of police brutality toward other citizens of the United States. If anything, the evidence is abundant in the other direction. The murdering of policemen year by year and the ever-mounting assaults on our symbols and enforcers of law and order suggest that rather than police brutality toward the public, there is a steadily building wave, veritably a tidal wave, of "people brutality" toward the police.

Singularly enough, if the anti-police forces were to win out and establish the kind of anarchical society they appear to want, it is they, not the majority of people, who would be in danger. For the anti-policeman, the Communist, the beatnik, peacenik, and general variety of nitwitnik, including the college boy who believes the right of free speech carries with it a concomitant right to spit in the eye of the law, are woefully in the minority and might well be the target of a vengeful majority were anarchy to reign in the United States.

Be all that as it may, when is a policeman "brutal?"

Under the law, both Federal and state, the officer has a right to use whatever force is "reasonably necessary" in making an arrest. The arrest, though, may not be based on mere whim. It must be for "probable cause."

Furthermore, the policeman, just like any other citizen, has the right of self-defense. If he is attacked by anyone, including someone already in custody, he has a right to use whatever force is necessary to protect himself. The officer likewise may use whatever force is necessary to prevent the escape of a suspect. Generally speaking, this would, rather naturally, include the shooting of an escaping suspect if there was no other way to prevent his escape.*

Conversely, certain laws or rules and regulations make the policeman liable to punishment if more than "reasonable force" is used against an individual. Besides the possibility of departmental trials for using more force than is needed or for assaulting another citizen, let us say, without provocation, the policeman may be subject to prosecution under state and Federal laws. He has no right to punish anyone; and

---

* One notable execption to this general statement is Section 35.30 of the New York State Revised Penal Law, which took effect September 1, 1967. Under the new law, which may well be amended in the 1968 session of the Legislature since it has evoked so many anguished and angry outcries, a policeman in New York State may use deadly physical force in effecting an arrest or in preventing a escape only if "he reasonably believes such force is necessary to defend himself or a third person from what he reasonably believes to be the use or imminent use of deadly physical force" or if he "reasonably" believes the suspect or escaper has committed or attempted to commit a felony involving the use of deadly physical force; is attempting to escape by using a deadly weapon; or otherwise indicates that he is likely to endanger human life or to inflict serious physical injury unless apprehended without delay.

Section 35.20 of the same revised statute, on the other hand, takes away the home owner's right to defend his own castle. Under its dictates, a home owner may not use deadly physical force against an intruder unless the latter threatens the home owner with deadly physical force; or is "using or about to use physical force against an occupant of a dwelling while committing or attempting to commit a burglary of such dwelling"; or is "committing or about to commit kidnaping, robbery, forcible rape, or forcible sodomy"; or is attempting to commit arson.

Thus, it would appear that a father would be justified in shooting an intruder in the act of forcibly raping his three-year-old daughter in the home, but would be totally and completely unjustified is using deadly physical force against the intruder *if the act had already been committed* and the intruder was escaping from the home.

f he does use more force than indicated by the circumstances, he may be held strictly accountable for his actions.

Also, there is the companion matter of civil liability. In some jurisdictions, at least, the municipality which employs him, not the policeman himself, is held liable for damages in any civil suit arising out of he "wrongful" action of a policeman.

Thus, in a New York State case some years ago where persons complained that a man inside a house was threatening them with a loaded rifle, the policeman who entered the house and shot the man dead (and the man did indeed have a loaded rifle) saw a jury bring in a verdict of $80,000 against the municipality under whose jurisdiction he policeman came.

There were complicated legal questions involved—the lack of a search warrant, etc.—but there is little doubt that the jury considered the policeman guilty of having used poor judgment, extremely poor judgment, in this case.

In another "poor judgment" case, a policeman chasing a suspect in an allegedly stolen car took aim and shot at one of the tires of the fleeing car. The trouble was that the policeman put the bullet through the closed window of his patrol car. The slug went wild, penetrated the kickplate of a storm door, and pierced the leg of a housewife who had come to the door on hearing the screeching of brakes.

The jury's verdict: $15,000 for the injured housewife against the county which employed the policeman.

By itself, this kind of poor judgment has nothing to do with brutality, although there are undoubtedly situations in which "brutality" charges actually stem from the exercise of poor judgment. If all of us were completely moral and were endowed with the ability to make correct judgments in all situations, however, we would need neither laws nor policemen. But the human being is not so gifted. Nor will he ever be.

An examination of some of the statistics vis-a-vis police "brutality" charges proves exceedingly interesting. According to the U. S. Department of Justice, between the middle of 1964 and mid-1965, there were 1,700 complaints of police brutality referred to the FBI. Included were civil rights complaints in the South. Of 47 cases presented to Federal grand juries, only five led to convictions.

Similarly, in many United States cities the bulk of complaints of police brutality are proved unfounded or dismissed after investigation or hearings. In one period in Chicago, for example, 289 complaints against police were received. In all, 274 were either "not sustained" or judged to be "unfounded." Complete exoneration resulted in eight cases, while seven were sustained, and the officers involved were disciplined.

In Washington, D. C. only sworn complaints against policemen receive official recognition. As a consequence, the reluctance of people to take oath knocks out many of the complaints at the very beginning.

If Philadelphia was the first to establish a civilian-dominated police review board (its Police Advisory Board was established by Mayor Richardson Dilworth in 1958), it also was the first to have a court abolish its board. In late March, 1967, Common Pleas Judge Leo Weinrot ruled that the board was illegal and must be abolished. In his landmark decision, which the city promptly announced it would appeal, Judge Weinrot held that the Fraternal Order of Police, which had initiated the suit, had amply proved that the board, in particular cases, impaired police morale, hindered police in the performance of their duties, and drove "some of them to think of leaving the force."

Said Judge Weinrot. "The very existence of the board, the harassment of officers, and the anxiety which its existence promotes must inevitably lessen the effectiveness of police performance." He added that the very existence of the board menaced law enforcement and public welfare.

From 1958 through 1965, the board had received 804 complaints. On 210 of them, they handed down decisions. In all, 320 cases were withdrawn, settled without hearings, or closed for failure of the complainants to appear; 106 were still awaiting investigation, and 68 were awaiting board hearings.

There can be practically no question that the specter of civilian review boards lessens police morale; hence increases crime by diminishing police effectiveness.

During the fierce campaign waged for and against the Mayor John V. Lindsay-backed civilian police-review board in New York City in 1966, some policemen told me they were taking the easy way out. Many of them had taken civil service examinations for the Fire Department and when certified for appointment were simply going to bow out of the Police Department and join the fire-fighters. "Nobody picks on the fireman for doing his job," one policeman told me.

When the New York City civilian review board was overwhelmingly defeated by a margin of over half a million votes in 1966, the people of New York City showed, in my opinion, that they were

houlder to shoulder with their policemen in standing for law and or-
er in a city sorely in need of nothing but.

To advert to just one phase of that hot campaign, the gaping
redibility gap implicit in the charge by the Lindsay forces that the
o-called "sleeper clause" in the referendum on the civilian review
oard would insulate the police from investigation for their acts was
bout as evident as the maw of the Grand Canyon. New York City
olice today, as then, are just as liable to have to answer to grand
uries, to courts, and to others for their actions if they exceed their
awful authority.

(Incidentally, "credibility gap" is a euphemism invented by poli-
icians to sugar-coat what might otherwise be termed an outrageous
ie.)

Despite all the dire predictions of supporters of the civilian-domi-
ated police review board, little beyond the membership of the board
as changed in New York City. According to a report released in
March, 1967, by the city's new police review board, which consists of
wo deputy police commissioners and three civilian members of the
Police Department, the civilian-dominated group which the voters
lisestablished in November, 1966, had received 444 complaints from
une 30 to November 8. Of those, the board disposed of 146, recom-
nending the preferring of charges in four cases. The present board,
which came into being in late November, 1966, received 282 complaints from that time until March, 1967, and handled 123. Just five
f those resulted in recommendations that charges be preferred against
he policemen involved. Therefore, although the civilian-dominated
oard received more complaints in a fairly comparable period, it rec-
mmended disciplinary action in one fewer case than the self-policing
olice board, almost too insignificant a difference to be any difference
t all.

(As a matter of fact, a later report indicated an upsurge of cases
n April, 1967, demonstrating increasing public confidence in the pres-
nt police-dominated review board.)

The types of police brutality charges made merit some mention.
Frequently, as FBI Director Hoover has pointed out, charges are
nade not to lawful authority, but to newspapers and other media or
re the main topic at outdoor-rally harangues or are even the subject
f loud plaints from the pulpit. Another means is through the medium
f the printed pamphlet, with rarely any proof to back up the charges.

The filing of false charges with the police is in itself a crime, and prosecution of the offender can ensue. This possibility may explain why the "victims" of "police brutality" simply neglect to file their charges with official bodies which might take action against the alleged offending officer.

Many of the "brutality" charges are really a form of "verbal brutality." Apparently some members of the public believe they have every right to "cuss out" a policeman, but he in turn is a brute and a beast if he answers his critics in the same terms.

That complaints of police brutality can border on the ludicrous is attested to by the charges lodged with the U. S. Department of Justice by a Southern Negro woman who claimed that her son had been abused simply for stealing a bag of peanuts. Subsequent investigation revealed that the burlap bag of peanuts the son "stole" just happened to be in a trailer truck which the son—obviously needing something in which to transport the peanuts—also stole.*

There is no doubt that there are, as Mr. Hoover has conceded, isolated incidents of irresponsible and brutal conduct on the part of police officers. But there likewise is no doubt that the "police brutality" gambit has been overplayed, for a very obvious purpose: If a lie is pounded into the consciousness of the populace often enough, eventually it will be considered gospel. Actually, the picture of people being bludgeoned, harassed, or third-degreed at every turn is about as truthful a reflection of naked fact as are the false-faces children wear on Halloween.

But the false-faced charge of police brutality or what is taken on the spur of the moment by minority groups especially to be police brutality can have deadly consequences. Let us not forget—who could?—that it was the attempt of a police officer to arrest a Negro on a charge of drunken driving that provided the lightning spark which caused the flames of racial wrath to consume a goodly portion of the Watts section of Los Angeles in 1965. Before order was restored, 30 persons, including two peace officers, were killed; and 895 persons, 90 peace officers among them, were injured.

Significantly, the man whose arrest had touched off the riot pleaded guilty to the drunken-driving charge. Despite that fact, the cry of "police brutality" was used to excuse away the orgy of uncontrollable mob brutality which resulted in arson, looting, and mayhem of all sorts.

---

* See *Police "Brutality," U. S. News & World Report,* Sept. 6, 1965.

If it is agreed that a sadist may sometimes be able to join a police department, just as the arsonist at times has a flare for firemanic pursuits—literally setting fires for pay until he's caught—it can by no means be admitted that the sadist is the prototype of the presentday policeman. On the contrary, the average policeman today is a responsible individual. He not only regards himself a professional; he tries to comport himself as a professional. He knows that he must at all times endeavor to remain courteous, calm, collected, coolheaded in the most nerve-frazzling situations. Consider, for example, the times the officer must endure extreme provocation in particularly high-crime neighborhoods where physical danger oftentimes lurks in forbidding alleys, dark doorways, poorly lighted streets.

Still, despite this state of affairs, as former Chicago Police Superintendent O. W. Wilson in his book, *Police Administration,* has pointed out: "The officer . . . must remember that there is no law against making a policeman angry and that he cannot charge a man with offending him. Until the citizen acts overtly in violation of the law, he should take no action against him, least of all lower himself to the level of the citizen by berating and demeaning him in a loud and angry voice. The officer who withstands angry verbal assaults builds his own character and raises the standards of the department."

As the President's Crime Commission report acknowledges, "all responsible police officials subscribe to those views, and departments have regulations prescribing discourteous and courteous behavior by its members, although in many departments the regulations are unspecific."

Virtually all police departments of any size at all have adequate machinery to weigh complaints of "brutality" and to punish the offending officer if the evidence shows him to be guilty of a brutality charge. Some departments even employ psychiatrists in an attempt to keep sadistic or emotionally unfit persons out of their departments. That the screening methods used cannot be 100 percent effective I nothing doubt. No yardstick yet devised by mortal man can accurately measure the mentality of human beings. I have stenographically recorded too much diametrically opposed testimony of psychiatrists—one psychiatrist claiming a man is insane and the other just as stoutly proclaiming that he is not—to believe otherwise.

Should we have civilian review boards to police our police? The people of the City of New York certainly didn't think so when they administered a sledgehammer blow to that idea in November, 1966. If that one referendum isn't persuasive enough as a reason for not having civilian review boards, how about the surveys in such places as the slum areas of Watts and New York City's Harlem which demonstrated that the prime concern of most families is "crime in the streets" and the "need for more police protection," *not* "police brutality."

The policeman has been caught up in a social revolution. He is a whipping boy for architects of social change. But he's not as mayhem-minded, generally, as the "law-abiders" who toss bottles and bricks at him from rooftops or who try to run him down with just about as lethal a weapon as the fiendish mind of man ever invented—the automobile.

Transcending in importance all these reasons for not having non-policemen policing the police we have the little matter of police morale. If law and order is to prevail in America—and it must if we are to survive as a nation—then we must have policemen with enough resolve to carry out their duties. The public can never be sure that the policeman has that necessary resolve unless it supports him to the hilt.

When New York City's civilian review board campaign was just about at its hottest in October, 1966, I heard of the policeman who saw five men having a free-for-all in a parking lot. The officer was alone. As he said later, he could have summoned help and waited until it arrived or he could have taken the easy way out: not only to *look* the other way, but to *go* the other way.

He chose the latter course. "If I waded in and tried to stop that fight and was attacked by these men," he said, "I might have had to use my gun to protect myself. I couldn't take that chance. So I simply left."

That one incident underscores the demoralizing influence civilian review boards have on the man most responsible for preserving law and order in the United States.

One must reluctantly admit the officer had a point. No civilian review board could possibly say he acted wrongly if he took no action at all and if his *failure to act* was never brought to their attention.

Nevertheless, if that is a sample of the kind of morale the very thought of civilian review boards instills in police and the type of protection review boards engender, then the Philadelphia judge who abolished the review board in that city gave all America something to think of when he said that the destruction of police morale by civilian review boards menaces law enforcement and public welfare.

It does precisely that. When a man can loot a store while a police nan stands by helplessly unable to take any action or *ordered* to take no action, something is outrageously wrong not only *in* America but *with* America. Still, it's never too late to make things right. And civilian review boards are not the answer.

The decisive voice of an aroused people ready to do battle with the evil forces abroad in our land is the one answer, the only answer, to crime in the United States.

CHAPTER SEVEN

The Family and the Policeman

"I WOULD RATHER sentence a convicted man to prison than sit in judgment on a writ of habeas corpus involving the custody of children."

So spoke a judge in open court some years ago. He went on to declaim that warring parents in their frenzy to "get even" with one another literally tear the lives of their children apart, not to say what they do to their own peace of mind.

Much more, ever so much more damage is done by battling parents to their children than they do to each other. They shatter their children's emotions, and most importantly, they destroy their faith in the family as a unit. In children especially love and respect for family—faith—should, like a flower, be nurtured until it reaches the full bloom of maturity.

If some judges aren't exactly ecstatic about attempting to be Solomonic in deciding where justice lies in matrimonial disputes, what about the police officer who often must act like a father confessor or a referee in a serious matrimonial "engagement" which might—and sometimes does—result in murder or mayhem unless the police intervene?

I asked a policeman friend, "What is the first thought that pops into your head when you're called upon to go to a home in which the husband and wife are having a whale of a scrap?"

With a wry smile, he answered, "Impulse tells me to go in the other direction. But I don't. I go where I'm ordered, and I just hope it's the case of a husband with a bit too much under his belt. Usually you can reason with that kind. You ask him to leave the house with you, and after protesting several times that 'Everything's all right; I haven't done a thing,' he'll leave with you."

"What about children?" I asked. "Do these fighting couples generally have children?"

"They do. And it's a helluva life for them to see their parents tear-

ng the hearts out of one another day after day. Remember, some of
these fights go on for years."

"You know," I said, "I've often wondered what happened to children who from infancy to the day they reached maturity and got out
of the house witnessed intermittent, never-ending battles between
their parents. I wonder whether there have ever been any studies along
that line?"

"Don't know," my friend replied, "but the chances are always
good that they'll end up the same way if they get married. After all,
they haven't seen anything else all their lives."

"Not necessarily," I said. "If they're bright kids, they may very
well have the thought literally knocked into them that there's something better in this old world than getting married and snapping at
one another's throat for the rest of one's life."

"What do people like this gain?" the officer asked. "They gain
nothing. Their children gain nothing."

"They reap the reward of misery, sometimes lifelong misery," I
answered, "and I think I've seen the prototype of all matrimonial
cases."

I thought of the "liquored up" husband who tried to bayonet his
wife with a Japanese war souvenir as she sat in an overstuffed chair.
He wound up impaling the chair when the wife jumped up and out of
the way. I remembered the husband who used his wife as a punching
bag. And the shrew who made her husband's life a hell on earth for
37 agonizing years until the day he put on his hat and walked out of
her life forever.

"Without violating any confidences," I said, "can you tell me in
general terms about any case of a matrimonial dispute which you
think makes a rather significant point?"

The officer thought a moment. "Well, without mentioning names or
locale, there's this couple who's always fighting. At least once a week,
almost without fail, we're summoned to their house, usually by the
wife, but once the husband himself phoned claiming his wife was
threatening him with a knife. I think he wanted to turn the tables on
her. Anyhow that's one call we all dread making."

"Why?" I asked.

"Well, practically every time as the responding officer tries to restore peace and harmony while they're screaming at each other, the
poor guy winds up being the goat. They suddenly turn on the officer,
both of them, and vent their anger on the man who's actually there

at the invitation of one of the battlers. I don't know how many times I've been ordered out of that house."

"I guess that kind of thing makes you bitter?" I suggested.

He laughed. "Not at all. Once they start turning their rage on me, I figure they're getting together again. When they zero in on me I think it's a subconscious effort on their part to save face. So I save face too—my own—which I try to keep straight as I retreat. I reason that after I'm gone they'll kiss and make up, and peace will descend on that household once more for the rest of the night. It usually does."

"By the way, are they drinkers?"

"No," he replied. "They're just fighters. And they have children, three of them. But they never stop to think of how they may be wrecking their *children's* lives. None of them ever do."

"What's the answer, a marriage counselor?"

"Maybe, but I doubt it. Chances are they'd wind up fighting with the marriage counselor."

This time I laughed in spite of myself. My mind swung back to that classic case of the dueling duo that had "fought the good fight" for 35 long years. Decades-long veterans of the courts, both should have been experts in matrimonial law by that time. They appeared to derive masochistic pleasure from visiting all sorts of verbal and physical abuse on one another. When the wife wailed on the witness stand that her husband had physically assaulted her, hospital records were produced proving that she herself had fractured her husband's skull not once, but twice over the years. In fact, the proof showed that he had been patched up at hospitals on many other occasions as well.

Why didn't this tussling couple acquire a legal separation or a divorce and have done with the matter? Simply because, as I viewed the situation, they enjoyed fighting, particularly with each other, too much to think of ever parting.

What does the policeman do when confronted by situations which, as former New York City Police Commissioner Murphy has said, he did not cause and cannot really solve? As my officer friend indicated, he tries to take the husband, usually treated as the villain of the piece, for a walk to give him a chance to cool down. Or perhaps the policeman will suggest that the enraged husband bed down in a hotel for the night, thereby giving tempers on both sides an opportunity to abate.

The crazed husband with a loaded shotgun is quite another matter. If he's threatening to kill his wife and anyone else who comes within range, he presents a rather formidable problem.

"What do you do in those cases?" I asked my friend.

"Those are the bad ones," he said. "You just pray a little; that's all. If you can get close enough, you try to talk to the man and reason with him, asking him to drop his weapon. If he starts pegging shots at you, you can't take any more chances. There's a shoot-out. You have to try to get him before he kills somebody."

"Peace officers sometimes get killed in such situations, don't they?"

"They do." My friend shrugged. "It's part of the job."

Policemen are not supermoralists. They're probably no more honest, really, than the average member of society. Yet, like a church which stands as a symbol of the belief in God, they stand for morality. They stand for honesty. They stand for proper codes of conduct on the part of all men, women, and children in their relationships with one another. If at times a policeman reflects the morality of large segments of society and is caught committing a dishonest act, it is his uniform he dishonors, not the idea or ideal behind it.

As enunciated heretofore, the policeman is usually a family man who knows something of the give and take of married life and of the necessity of keeping family units intact if we are to indeed have a good society, a clean society, an orderly society.

In discussing the importance of the family as a moral influence, I cannot help but think of the courageous words of the policeman's wife, the mother of six children, who was told that her husband would probably never walk again. He had been paralyzed from the waist down by a bullet fired by a man involved in a family ruckus. That plucky wife and mother said, according to the press: "You're not giving me bad news. You're telling me that he will live and I can have him with me again. No, no, this is good news."

If all families displayed courage of that superb quality in the face of adversity almost beyond compare, this country would likely never need matrimonial courts or lawyers to try matrimonial disputes or marriage counselors or family service agencies.

Some persons regard the tendency to indict society as a whole for the rising crime rate in America as oversimplifying the cause of a very complex problem. To some extent it probably is. But if our societal makeup is dissected and the forces that are at work sundering the moral fabric of our nation, corrupting the young, and promoting anarchy in our midst are minutely examined, the most fair-minded among us can only honestly conclude that society is truly and accurately to blame for the soaring crime rate in the United States.

Prayer has been banned from our schools, while obscenity in its ugliest, filthiest forms has received the blessing of the very court that has banned prayer—the Supreme Court of the United States. It prefers to strike down, not build up, the religious influence in America.

If economic conditions are a cause for crime—and they are, though affluence will by no means deter the crooked-minded from attempting to acquire greater affluence—not enough is done to wipe out the economic conditions which are at least one of the causes of crime. Ghettos remain ghettos, though some attempt at rebuilding —structures, not humans necessarily—is made.

On the other hand, unemployment insurance is paid *to keep people unemployed,* not to insure gainful employment.

What would stop a government which doles out unemployment insurance of, say, $50 a week from saying to industry: "Tell you what, gentlemen, we'll pay *you* $50 a week for X amount of weeks to keep this presently unemployed man *on the job* if you'll add enough to it to give him a living wage. Maybe by the end of the stipulated period you'll be able to absorb him into your operations and increase your own productive capacity by that much, without any further help from government."

Is this idea socialistic? Hardly. Certainly no more socialistic than paying out insurance to keep people *out of work.* And if increasing production and profits by plans like this is wrong, then I'm happy to be wrong.

At any rate, let's change "unemployment insurance" to "employment insurance." Change it from a negative to a positive in this country, and you'll work wonders not only by increasing productivity and the chance of profits, but by giving the unemployed a sense of dignity and an opportunity for self-respect often denied them by the "do-gooding" forces of government.

Governments cannot legislate the good life, as the adherents of the "Great Society" have been attempting. They cannot say, "We believe the family is the backbone of our nation. Therefore, we want all families to stay together to make their lives more meaningful."

Or perhaps they could say it. But their words would fall on stone-deaf ears.

Any attempt at reinstituting morality and spirituality in America must come from within the societal structure itself. If the people want less crime, they must insist upon the moral life. If they would direct their children along the paths of rightness and righteousness, they must be leaders, not permissive followers, of youngsters not old enough to exercise proper self-judgment.

If gangs are kindred to families in that they give their members a sense of identity, a sense of belonging, which the child without family or loving friends secretly longs for, doesn't that knowledge alone speak eloquently for the preservation of the family unit in America? To me, the youth who joins a gang acquires a family. It may be a "family" composed exclusively of black sheep, but it's a kind of family nevertheless. For whatever else its characteristics, the gang is a group of unhappy youths drawn together not by the bonds of friendship, but by the bonds of unhappiness, the need to lean upon one another for mutual support. Simply by joining a gang, the member makes one tacit concession: He can't face life alone.

The members of a happy family, conversely, feel no such need. They are at peace with society and, more importantly, at peace with each other. Consequently, none of their members is likely to become a problem to society.

The family is indeed the backbone of any nation. Without it, we would all breed like rabbits; morality, as bad as it is today, would be virtually non-existent; and in that sort of dissolute society we would be ready prey for any "ism" that craved to devour us.

Still, there are forces at work in our country that are softening the backbone of society by actively helping to destroy families and the sense of security that a happy family life gives to the growing child.

Divorce laws, already too flexible, are making it steadily easier for a child to have two or three or more fathers in his lifetime: his own, real father and one or two or more stepfathers as a mother bounces from marriage to marriage like a rubber ball.

Organizations, many of them charitable and religious, take over the responsibilities of unwed parents by caring for or adopting out children of such irresponsible "parents," who then are free to repeat the cycle all over again.

"Boy states he has two fathers," the school record read. Maybe he was lucky; some children have more.

Probably the greatest irony of all is the case of the divorced couple, each since remarried, who come storming into court protesting their love for the offspring of their former union. Actually, if they really had loved their children when it counted most, they would have tried their uttermost to have compromised their differences, making the best of a rocky marriage for their children's sake as well as their own, thereby giving the words of the marriage ceremony, "till death do us part," the meaning they used to and still should have.

In better than a quarter century as a court stenographer, I don't think I've heard of a case more tragicomical than that of the boy friend who came into court seeking visitation rights with his child born to somebody else's wife.

It seems that while the husband was in jail, the boy friend moved into the home of the wife in question. In the natural—or unnatural—course of events, the woman had a baby, courtesy of the boy friend, not the husband. When the husband was released from jail, he evinced a quality of understanding beyond the pale of believability: He barred the boy friend from his home, but kept the child and forgave his wife.

Soon afterward, the boy friend sued out a writ of habeas corpus demanding visitation rights with *his* child. And since he was the natural father, under the law he had a right to see his child. The court gave him that right away from the home of the legally married couple. After all, bloodshed might have, could have, and probably would have resulted if the boy friend had been given visitation rights at the home of the boy-friend-hating husband.

What's wrong with this type of situation, besides the great moral issue involved? First of all, why should not any man who sires a child out of wedlock be forced, by operation of law, to support that child to the best of his ability, even though the child be adopted by another couple, placed in a state institution, or in the home of foster parents? I strongly favor laws which would sentence able bodied unwed fathers to work, if they are not already gainfully employed, to support the children they bring into the world.

According to a reliable source, one New York State man is said to have fathered 30 children, all of them out of wedlock, and all of them public charges. Let us assume that this report is exaggerated and the harem-minded man in question only fathered 15 children or so. Whatever the number, is it in the interest of the public or in the interest of the unfortunate children brought into this world to have this sort of irresponsibility supported by the state? More bluntly, is it in the interest of the public to have welfare departments directly or indirectly supporting human studs?

I fully appreciate that the aim of welfare departments and of

haritable and religious organizations is to help the illegitimate child
n these situations. But I question whether it is really in the interest
f society as a whole and of the particular children, as well, to help
erpetuate immorality of this contemptibility in America.

Of course, any plan like this is difficult of fruition. Paternity
roceedings might have to be brought first against a man accused of
athering an unwanted child. Then, if a suitable agreement could not
e worked out whereby the father would voluntarily support the
hild until he or she reached the age of emancipation, a court could
old a hearing on the matter and sentence the father, if necessary, to
upport his own child.

This particular kind of "sentence to work" law should operate
even though the child is adopted out or placed in an institution or
the home of foster parents. Should support payments be as little as
$10 a week, they would nevertheless be a bonanza by the time the
child reached 18 or 21 and might well defray the expenses of a
college education.

Undeniably, the law cannot change a man into a responsible
human being overnight, if ever. But it can, through its sanctions,
plant the germ-seed of responsibility in an otherwise barren brain.

If the delinquent child, as some authorities contend, is more likely
to come from a family lacking moral and emotional authority over its
members or if deep unhappiness between parents increases the likeli-
hood of delinquency, it naturally follows that family ties have to be
strengthened, and the family must be recognized once more as the
institution which is the one stabilizing or normalizing influence in
the life of the child.

When parents lose control over their offspring, the outcome is
likely to be delinquent behavior on the part of the children who
fend for themselves because no adult gives them the proper sense of
direction.

The same is true of the school teacher who exercises little authority, hence has very little influence, over her charges.

Years ago a mother walked into a classroom. The place was a
bedlam. Children were talking and walking about, some were yelling
gleefully, others were sitting in their chairs or were perched on top
of desks. Horrified at the sight, the mother approached the teacher
and asked her why the class was in total disorder. The teacher
frowned. She spread her arms vertically and then horizontally as she

said dogmatically: "Children must grow this way and this way emotionally. Right now they're meeting their emotional needs."

The teacher was obviously a disciple of the "learn-by-doing" sect in the schools—learn by doing whatever you please. So what if this form of misdirection or undirection leads to incorrigibility and then criminality in later years. The teacher who planted the seeds will likely never know what kind of crop society will have harvested.

Like the happy family, the schools should have a stabilizing influence on children. Unhappily, that is not always the case.

Some years ago when I labored for a newspaper I asked a number of parents whether they thought the public schools fell down on the job, and if so, in what respect. They were practically unanimous in their response: Discipline, they said, was the one thing lacking in the public schools.

Discipline is the father of respect. Without the former, the latter is rarely present in the school setting.

The day I recorded the testimony of the young military school student proves the point. His manners were impeccable: "Yes, sir. No, sir. I beg your pardon, sir." I wondered how many public schoolchildren would evince that kind of respect for adults if they weren't disciplined to do it.

What can the schools do to help reinfuse order in a disorderly, crime-blighted society? They cannot instill love of God in the child —the U. S. Supreme Court has seen to that—but they can instill love of country and respect for this nation's institutions. They could even have courses in proper manners, proper attire, and orderly behavior. It might be an abrupt departure from the "gutter culture" so prevalent today, but it would be surpassingly interesting to see the uncouth youth transformed into an obedient, respectful member of society.

One way to get better discipline in the schools is to hire more male teachers, especially after about the third grade. Boys particularly resent women more than they do the "father figure." Why not employ men teachers pretty much exclusively from the fourth grade on—big, burly chunks of masculinity who can both speak and act with the voice of authority?

Says the President's Crime Commission in its 1967 initial report: "If one parent (especially the father of a son) is absent, if there are many children, if a child is in the middle in age among several siblings —such family arrangements tend to reduce parental control and uthority over children and consequently increase vulnerability to influences toward delinquent behavior."

The Crime Commission recognizes the value of the family as a force for good in the life of a child. Shouldn't the schools do likewise?

In high school classes, for instance, what would be wrong with courses on marriage taught not by teachers who may themselves be unhappily married or thrice divorced, but by experts in the field: family court judges, clergymen of all faiths, attorneys the bulk of whose practice has been in the matrimonial field, psychiatrists, and policemen themselves, all of whom could stress the desirability of keeping families intact and could show first-hand what happens to families that are torn apart.

Is it really asking too much to demand that the kind of morality engendered by the wholesome family life be taught in the schools? If God has been expelled, must morality also be barred?

A high school teacher I interviewed some time ago put this question to her class: "Which would you rather be, popular or honest?" She was aghast when most of the high schoolers answered, "Popular."

Actually, they were probably merely reflecting the general attitude of society: that popularity is much more important, much more to be desired, than honesty.

On the academic level, we all have seen too many examples of their failures to believe that the schools are doing on adequate job. The non-academically inclined student is nevertheless treated as though he had a "white collar" brain. Often he doesn't. And if he can't work with his head, let him work with his hands, *even in the early grades*. What good is a boy or a girl to society who repeatedly fails geometry, let us say, simply because it is beyond his or her intellectual capacity? And what does leaving him back do for him beyond branding him a dunce? Far better would it be to teach him something he has the capacity to learn, not to say the *will* to learn.

Again, the Crime Commission reports:

"Recent research has related instances of delinquent conduct to the school-child relationship and to problems either created or complicated by schools themselves. First, in its own methods and practices, the school may simply be too passive to fulfill its obligations as one of the last social institutions with an opportunity to rescue the child from other forces, in himself and in his environment, which are pushing him toward delinquency. Second, there is considerable evidence that some schools may have an indirect effect on delinquency by the use of methods that create the conditions of failure for certain students. Mishandling by the school can lower the child's motivation to learn. It can aggravate his difficulty in accepting authority and generate or intensify hostility and alienation. It can sap the child's confidence, dampen his initiative, and lead him to negative definitions of himself as a failure or an 'unacceptable person.'

"Some schools, particularly in the poorest areas, are unable to deal with children who are neither ready nor able to learn. Asserting demands for performance that the child cannot meet, the frustrated teacher may become hostile and the child indifferent, apathetic, or hostile in turn. If the child is also rebelling at home, the effect is more immediate and the confrontation becomes intolerable to all. The too-usual result is that the child turns to other things that have nothing to do with academic learning, and the school finds a way to ignore him or push him out so the rest of its work can continue."

There is an ever-burgeoning emphasis in the schools on psychological probing of the child's psyche. Some of the privacy-invading tests, the personality inventories particularly, help implant disrespect for family by putting to the child such indirect questions as:

"My father is a tyrant."

"There is constant bickering and quarreling in my home."

"I'm ashamed of my father's job."

"I'm ashamed of my parents' dress and manners."

If the schools' main purpose were to tear families apart and thereby help the forces that generate immorality in America, one might concede some value to these tests. But that is not the purpose of the schools, nor should it be.

The real purpose of the schools is to educate the child to the limits of his intellectual capacity, not to make a "white collar" pundit out of "blue collar" material.

Sometimes, too, we lose sight of the true purpose of education by overemphasizing the importance of college and pushing into college students who are not actual college material.

A college graduate said recently, "Well, I got my degree, but the only trouble I have now is that I can't find a job." If young men like these had the aptitude and didn't mind soiling their fingers, however, many "blue collar" jobs available today wouldn't go begging.

The child labor laws also need amending. At 14, a child should be permitted to get a job from which he may reap a return called self-respect as well as money. He should, as now in many areas, be permitted to deliver newspapers at 12 or even younger.

Idleness and indolence are two causes of crime. But the child busy earning money and self-esteem is not likely to be hanging around street corners figuring out ways to get into trouble.

The police too could help inculcate respect for authority by setting up speakers' bureaus whose members would go from school to school delivering addresses on the work of the policeman, what kinds of activity can get youths into trouble, and the ever-pressing need of the police for community cooperation if they are to do their job effectively.

Other ways can be found to strengthen family life in America and the individual member's feeling of dignity and self-importance. The President's Crime Commission advocates a re-examination and revision of welfare regulations so that they contribute to keeping families together. Actually, under some welfare regulations, a father has to leave the house in order for his family to receive assistance. How much better would it be if the welfare department stepped in, gave the family emergency help, and then did its utmost in attempting to get the father a job, or the mother if the father was ill or otherwise incapacitated and unable to work. The first and foremost requirement of welfare departments should be to *better* the welfare of the impoverished, not to demean them by keeping them on the dole forever.

In one period the Suffolk County, New York, Welfare Department reportedly saved the taxpayers about $350,000 by getting welfare recipients jobs and making them self-sustaining. In neighboring Nassau County, the presiding supervisor claimed in September, 1967, that some 500 persons had been removed from relief rolls, at a saving to the county of $450,000, through a re-training and job-placement program.

Multiply the total of those two figures, $800,000, by 1,000 counties all over the country and you have a saving of $800 million. Concomitantly, the savings in human dignity are incalculable.

These two counties are not particularly singular in their drive to get people off welfare rolls via the work-for-pay route. Similar efforts are being made in other states, and similar savings are being effected. Yet, the question remains: Is a total effort being made all over the United States to better the welfare of the employable through employment rather than a handout? The answer is, as it must be, a definite, unqualified NO.

In other respects welfare departments might well change their attitudes. Not too long ago a husband haled a welfare department into court on a writ of habeas corpus because he wanted custody of his children, who had been turned over to the department by his estranged wife. Rather than commending the man for his desire to face up to his responsibility and to be a father to his children, the welfare department *opposed* the application.

In a sense, all of us are policemen. Responsible parents "police" their children. Responsible public agencies should police themselves, always with due regard to the dignity of the members of the public with whom they have daily contact. And the police themselves should have, as the majority of them do, a professional attitude toward the public.

"I hate to arrest a kid," a policeman friend of mine said recently.

"I know," I said.

And I did know. The man is a father and he knows what it means for a youngster to get into trouble.

A former juvenile court judge told a group of people at a seminar that law officers should not be too eager to destroy juvenile gangs. While conceding that gangs may be responsible for some crime and delinquency, she argued that they "control their members to some extent, and there might be more crime without them." Without the support of his peers, his fellow gang members, she added, a youth might "retreat into himself, into drugs and alcohol. Which hurts society more?"

When youths have to gang up to seek "moral" support from one another, society has already been hurt. When children are ushered into the world by irresponsible parents who then desert them and when society supports this brand of irresponsibility, society not only is hurt; it is being self-destructive.

When the family unit is shattered by forces within our society, oftentimes aided and abetted by the "helping hand" of government, all the concepts of goodness, of decency, of law-abiding conduct engendered by the moralizing influences of family life are similarly destroyed.

Can the policeman police society? No, not really. It is society, in the final analysis, that must police itself. We must begin that process by letting a little of that old-fashioned quality called virtue seep back into our lives.

If virtue is its own reward, crime is the price we pay when we no longer permit it to be the guiding principle of our lives.

CHAPTER EIGHT

Ways to Combat Crime

AS A STRANGE HEAD poked its way through a window, the woman of the house was ready for the intruder. Down came her weapon, the common hammer: Wham! And out went the "lights" of a would-be burglar, rapist, or both.

The brave woman who nailed this suspect was not a member of Orlando's nationally famed, all-female "Pistol-Packing Posse." Yet, she nevertheless reflected the crime-spawned self-protective attitude that now prevails among women of that Central Florida city.

What triggered the formation of the crime-deterring Pistol-Packing Posse? During one period in 1966 there was a rapist plying his stealthy trade three or four times a week in Orlando, ordinarily a relatively quiet city. As is the case with so many of his ilk, the more defenseless the woman, the better. The rapist therefore preyed upon elderly women primarily, most of whom lived alone.

Perhaps it was the law of survival or maybe even a resurgence of old-fashioned instincts inherited from the rugged people who built this country; at any rate, gun sales suddenly zoomed to between 200 and 300 a week in Orlando, and women, not men, became the main buyers.

Parenthetically, in Orlando, a city of 90,000 persons, residents, as is true in most of Florida, may purchase firearms without restrictions.

Alarmed not so much by the abrupt upsurge in "gun-toting" by women, but by the uncomfortable thought that most of the purchasers hadn't the remotest idea about how to handle guns safely, the Orlando SENTINEL STAR conceived the idea of a police-trained "Pistol-Packing Posse."

Arrangemgents were made to invite the women to the Orlando Gun Club pistol range, where they would be taught how to handle and shoot guns by experts of the Orlando Police Pistol Team. The police expected that possibly 200 or 300 women would show for the first session in October, 1966; the SENTINEL STAR thought perhaps as many as 600 might appear. But to their mutual amazement, over 2,500 gun-carrying potential crime-busters came to the first session.

Ranging in age from 18 to 80, the "gunslingers" toted weapons of all descriptions in boxes, in pocketbooks, in holsters slung from hip-hugging slacks. Coeds, housewives, grandmothers, and great-grandmothers brought rifles, shotguns, Lugers, guns of World War I vintage, and modern, up-to-date guns of varying calibers and descriptions.

Nearly overwhelmed by the response, the Orlando Police Department was nonetheless capable of meeting the gun-training demand. It set up classes not once a week, as initially proposed, but three times a week, and limited them to 100 each, with trainees being scheduled by appointment.

With the accent on safety, the police weeded out the unusable guns, some of which hadn't been fired for 30 years or more. Women with aged or faulty weapons discarded them and were permitted to use police weapons in their stead.

Besides the Police Pistol Team, members of nearby McCoy Air Force Base have been assisting in the training. Short-range targets are used in the actual weapons-firing periods of instruction.

With the emphasis on safety, instructions include lessons in the proper loading and unloading, cleaning and storage of weapons. In fact, under the direction of Jack Stacey, Administrative Assistant to Chief of Police Carlisle Johnstone, a typewritten list of safety precautions has been issued. Besides instructing users in the proper cleaning and handling of guns, the list cautions gun owners to be especially careful in keeping guns out of the reach of children. It also pointedly tells gun owners and users never to aim at anything they do not intend to shoot.

The latter is a gun-use rule somewhat reminiscent of that, whether written or unwritten, prevailing in the U. S. Navy during World War II, when I stenographically reported many gunshot cases, including one in which a seaman used a .38-caliber revolver to play Russian roulette at mess table, with rather fatal consequences. The rule, as I recall it, in those days was: "Never draw your gun unless you are going to use it. But if you do, shoot to kill."

Up to March, 1967, membership in Orlando's Pistol-Packing Posse had swelled from an initial 2,500 to about 4,000; and more than 6,000 women had been trained in the proper handling and use of firearms.

Under Deputy Police Chief Stacey's leadership, classes have also been set up to instruct women in other self-protective ways. They are told how to protect themselves against assault, such as by making noise, parking in lighted areas, jabbing fingers in the assaulter's eyes, hitting their attacker in the groin and, above all, never being alone at night, in the first place, if at all possible.

Mr. Stacey, who cautions against using guns except "as a last resort for protection," also advocates better protection in the home through lighting, locks, chains on doors, and watchdogs. Again and again he emphasizes that guns should be kept away from children and from "immature or irresponsible people" as well. That the cautionary words are effective is proved out by the fact that there hadn't been a single known accident caused by any member of the Pistol-Packing Posse from the time of its inception until the spring of 1967, when this book was being written.

Substantial and varied are the reasons many women give for having joined the Pistol-Packing Posse. Said a 71-year-older: "With things the way they are these days, I want to be able to protect myself as best I can, so I'm here to learn all I can."

Another's interest was sparked by the fact that she was a victim of an attempted holdup in an Orlando parking lot. The police collared the would-be robber later on the basis of a description and a partial license plate number.

A third member explains the matter simply: "My husband is out of town a lot," she says, "and I feel I need the protection of knowing how to use a gun."

To date, the Pistol-Packing Posse program has produced many dividends. The crime rate has dropped rather spectacularly, although the police, by nature a conservative group, have ascribed the drop in part to the apprehension of the one man who, they charge, was committing most of the robberies and rapes of elderly women. Whether the police be conservative or no, the fact of the matter is that during the first six weeks after the gun-handling program got underway, there was only one attempted break-in in all of Orlando, that of the intruder nailed by the hammer-wielding woman. And in February, 1967, for the first time in two years, there was not a single assault, rape, or attempted rape of a woman in Orlando, Florida.

Again Deputy Chief Stacey says: "We do not claim our program is responsible (for the sudden total absence of these crimes), but the publicity given this program, we think, had a lot to do with this decrease."

To obliquely agree with Deputy Chief Stacey, there is little doubt that the would-be rapist would think twice or perhaps as much as ten times before attacking a woman who might be armed with a loaded gun which she knows how to use with lethal effect. To put it another way, the criminal who knows it's "open season" not on the victims of crime, but on its perpetrators, is indubitably a good deal less prone to carry on his "profession" with as much avidity as he may have previously demonstrated.

In a speech at Orlando College on October 28, 1966, Shirley Ann Gregersen summed up, in good measure, the general feeling of the "pistol-packing" women of that city. After thanking the Orlando police and the SENTINEL STAR for having cooperated in teaching "us poor, defenseless females how to handle firearms safely so that we would be able to protect ourselves against all types of criminals," she said: "I know that 2,500 women feel more secure in their homes at night because of these men."

The number then was 2,500. But as already stated, it has rocketed to 6,000 and is increasing all the time; for the program, the police say, will continue as long as interest in it remains alive.

The final unanticipated "reward" that the Orlando police have earned in teaching the women of their city modes of self-protection evidences itself in the increased respect Orlando citizens have for their Police Department. The image of the police officer in that Florida city is a good one, showing what crime-busting wonders can be worked when a concerned citizenry, an enlightened press, and a dedicated police force present a united front against the criminal element in an American city.

Apparently convinced that the "forearmed" female is an asset in deterring crime, the Orlando Police Department has issued a set of "organizational suggestions" for setting up similar pistol-packing posses elsewhere. It is doubtful that the idea will gain much acceptance in the North, however.

New York State's Sullivan Law, for example, which provides that anyone carrying concealable firearms have a license, also prohibits persons from keeping an unregistered pistol or revolver in his home or place of business without a license. In addition to state laws, many local ordinances carry similar provisions.

Even tear gas weapons are frowned upon in New York State. As a matter of fact, a young lady who used such a weapon on a man annoying her was convicted by a criminal court some months ago.

Since rape is a common crime in New York City and the city's 28,000 policemen cannot possibly protect millions of women from rapists and murderers, it almost seems incredible that the law should say to women, in effect: "No matter how often you are victimized by the criminal, no matter whether your very life may be in jeopardy, you may not defend yourself by carrying or owning any kind of un-licensed or unregistered concealable weapon which the law proclaims illegal."

Not all New York State legislators agree that women should remain defenseless "pigeons" because the law says so. State Senator Norman F. Lent of East Rockaway introduced a bill in the 1967 session of the New York State Legislature that would legalize the sale and possession of tear gas devices for self-defense purposes. Said the Senator: "To find a woman guilty of a violation of the Sullivan Law when her only intent was to repel a crime against her was a travesty on justice. I believe the use of the tear-gas device would act as a deterrent to would-be attackers who prey upon otherwise helpless citizens."

Despite the almost daily mugging, raping or murdering of women, sometimes even in the streets of New York, the Senator's plea fell on deaf ears. The State Senate tacitly told the women of New York that they must remain as defenseless as ever: It killed the bill.

Concededly, since President John F. Kennedy's assassination, there has been a concerted drive to outlaw all guns in this country. The present President's Crime Commission doesn't go that far. It does recommend, though, that all handguns, rifles, and shotguns be registered and that each state require a person to obtain a permit before he can either possess or carry a handgun.

It is desirable that all persons who own handguns or even rifles or shotguns be required to prove that they know how to handle such weapons. Most importantly, they should be taught to respect the gun. I have stenographically reported too many gunshot cases where the victim was guilty of sheer carelessness to believe otherwise.

Only three states, New York being one of them, outlaw tear gas devices now. All others allow persons, mostly women, to carry the devices around with them as a means of self-protection.

Would the complete outlawing of weapons, particularly guns, curb crime in America? This citizen doesn't think so. Were guns completely outlawed, a vast underground bootleg market in guns and knives, if need be, would likely spring up.

Furthermore, it is doubtful that guns could be successfully outlawed from another point of view. Many boys today know how to fashion their own (they can make zip guns out of car radio aerials, for instance), and the making of knives out of bits of steel would be mere child's play. Moreover, the adult criminal element would discern big profits in guns and would speedily devise ways of manufacturing them surreptitiously to fill the illicit, black-market demand.

In the final analysis, outlawing guns may be likened to Prohibition: People just won't obey any law they regard as too oppressive.

Besides, there are allegedly 100 million guns in this country, not counting those owned by the military forces. One wonders just how many Americans would willingly give up their weapons in a country in which the criminal is increasingly being pampered while his victim is largely ignored.

At any rate, while the quarrel rages over the licensing or outright prohibition of weapons, women in eight other American cities, some undoubtedly inspired by the pistol-packing women of Orlando, have been or are undergoing training in the use of firearms for self-defense. Though some programs have been sponsored by local business groups or other interested citizens, most of the programs are under the supervision of local police departments, sheriff's offices, or public safety departments. The eight other cities are: New Orleans, Louisiana; Ocala and Tampa, Florida; Shawnee, Kansas; Oklahoma City, Oklahoma; suburban Seattle, Washington; Huntsville, Alabama; and San Diego, California.

The crime-deterrent aspect implicit in a growing army of women schooled and skilled in the use of firearms is unquestionable; for what would-be rapist or burglar has the kind of courage it would take to steal into a home in the wee hours of the night with the knowledge that his head my be blown off by someone who not only has a gun, but knows how to use it with deadly effect?

In the face of the scandalously high rape rate in New York, some police departments have adopted new or at least previously untried techniques to apprehend the rapist or would-be rapist. Reacting sharply to the steadily climbing number of vicious attacks upon women since January 1, 1967, including the case of a 69-year-old woman who had both her arms broken by her attacker, the Nassau

County Police Department instituted a system previously tried in New York City. They decoyed a policeman decked out in women's clothes and a scarlet wig. For a time, 16 similarly garbed policemen walked the streets in trouble areas. The police worked in teams of two, the "woman" being kept under surveillance by a plainclothesman.

Patrolman Kenneth Krassner, disguised in slacks, a fur coat and red wig covered by a kerchief, drew first blood as he patrolled the streets of Westbury, Long Island, on Saturday, January 28. At about 6:30 P. M., a man stole up behind him, grabbed him, hauled him into an alley, and repeatedly slugged him with a cobblestone. Before he lost consciousness, the 180-pound policeman managed to draw his revolver and to shoot his assailant twice. Krassner's partner, Patrolman John Nabet, had seen his fellow officer disappear. As he rushed after him to investigate, he heard the shots ring out. Nabet made the arrest, but not without a struggle. Despite his wounds, the would-be woman molester put up the fight of a cornered animal.

Both Krassner and his assailant were taken to the hospital, the patrolman with a fractured skull and face cuts, his attacker with bullets in the chest and leg.

Sometimes real, honest-to-goodness women are used as decoys to nab the crime-bent in high-crime neighborhoods. Margaret Maloney, a policewoman, acted as a decoy in a plush New York City apartment. As she lolled in the apartment resplendent in a black slip and a red housecoat, a man who allegedly climbed into the apartment pounced on her. A detective, also part of the stake-out, shot the man, and a fellow officer was wounded as the bullet tore through the intruder's chest.

The stake-out had been set up because of complaints of "sexual assaults" in the neighborhood.

The police resort to other forms of deception in their interminable battle against crime. In New York City police officers often drive taxicabs because the taxi driver is a frequent crime victim.

All in all, whether policemen act as decoys dressed in women's clothes or as bogus taxicab drivers, their assignments are dangerous ones which nevertheless reap good returns in the number of robbers, including purse snatchers, and rapists, who are taken into custody.

Just as many women of Orlando have deputized themselves in the fight against crime in their city, other citizens can aid the police by becoming anti-crime fighters. Many of them already have.

Chicago can claim credit as the birthplace of an anti-crime drive called "CRIME-STOP." Organized by then Chicago Police Superintendent O. W. Wilson three years ago, it is a simple but effective system by which citizens actively support their police merely by pledging to become involved in the anti-crime war.

How does the system work? A citizen who spots a suspicious person or a crime actually in process quickly dials an emergency police number, and the response is almost instantaneous. The call goes directly to a prowl car dispatcher, who, in a matter of seconds, dispatches a patrol car to the area. In one instance, a patrol car reached the scene 40 seconds after a woman had made an urgent call.

Chicago's citizen crime-stoppers have a set of printed instructions. Terse and to the point, they advise the citizen to give the police (1) the address of the incident; (2) the number of persons involved; (3) a description of the scene and suspects (including such details as height, weight, age, complexion, and clothing); and (4) the license number of any car or cars involved.

CRIME-STOP, which has spread to other cities—in Detroit it's called IMPACT; in Kansas City, CRIME ALERT; in St. Louis, CITIZENS AGAINST CRIME—has figured in cutting the Chicago crime rate. In 1965, as an example, Chicago's crime rate plummeted 12 percent, while that of twenty-two other large cities rose by 4 percent.

True, with every citizen a self-deputized policeman, police departments are bound to receive a lot of "false alarms" from well-meaning citizens. But policemen generally don't mind checking out some false leads, for they know that a public on the side of the law and order is a tremendous aid on two counts: first, because of the proffered help; and second, because of the interest thereby evinced by citizens in *their* police department.

Many authorities have recognized the need for "citizen soldiers" in the war against crime. The Crime Commission, for one, has pointed out that every time a citizen fails to report on offense, he contributes his "mite to crime."

As already indicated, not all citizens are loath to enlist on the side of law and order in this perennial struggle. In 1962, just one day after a 90-year-old woman had been struck on the head and robbed on a public street, 30 Indianapolis women met to blueprint ways to make the streets of their city safer. The organization, called the Anti-Crime Crusade, has no dues, no membership cards, no bylaws, no minutes. But it is now 50,000 women strong and has 14 divisions.

Its concerted campaign has resulted in improved street lighting. It has helped young people get jobs, has urged and helped school dropouts to return to school, has involved thousands of adolescents in volunteer work for social service agencies and clinics, and has organized campaigns for cleaning up the slums.

Also, the Anti-Crime Crusade has sponsored police recruits, has observed the operation of the courts and publicized their shortcomings, has helped parole officers with their work, has campaigned for higher police pay, and has formed block clubs to improve slum neighborhoods.

In short, this energetic group has graphically demonstrated what a concerned citizenry can do if it rolls up its sleeves and willingly gets involved in worthwhile civic work which can—and does—help reduce crime.

The war against crime through economic means—getting employables off relief rolls and into gainful employment; changing *unemployment* insurance into *employment* insurance; modifying child labor laws to permit youngsters of 14 to work full time, if necessary—has already been detailed and needs no further elaboration here.

Other means of combating crime have likewise been touched on. Street lighting is all-important. Once you bathe the criminal in light, a bath not at all to his liking, he loses a formidable ally. For that reason alone, not to mention traffic considerations, street lighting should be improved wherever necessary throughout the nation.

Lighting is equally vital in the home. It's therefore a good plan to keep at least one light on all night in the home as a partial deterrent to crime.

Other simple, yet highly useful, steps can be taken to prevent crime. As noted, women should go out alone as infrequently as possible, especially at night and in strange neighborhoods. All police callboxes could well be made public callboxes to give citizen users practically instantaneous contact with the police in any kind of emergency.

Car theft is a major crime in America; yet, many thefts could be prevented. According to FBI statistics, the key had either been left in the ignition or the ignition had been left unlocked in 42 percent of all stolen cars in a given period. Two effective expedients can quickly reduce this percentage: failing to leave the keys in the car and making sure the ignition is locked when you leave it.

On the dope-pushing front, some states are taking steps at insuring quick treatment for the drug addict. Though many persons may have serious reservations about the effectiveness of these programs, they are at least a start. Any success they attain will have the concomitant value of relieving police of the burden of seeking out and apprehending unfortunates who turn to crime to get money for dope.

The cost of drugs is phenomenally high, so it is only logical that the addict turns to crime to keep himself supplied.

In April, 1967, a young man who voluntarily committed himself to the care and custody of the New York State Narcotic Addiction Control Commission admitted to a court that he used from eight to ten bags of heroine a day, at $5 a bag. This youngster had not been charged with any crime, but the $40 to $50 a day needed to sate his involuntary craving could easily have had other dire consequences in time.

Some states also are tightening laws as regards dope pushers. The pusher who is not himself an addict is neither more nor less than a mass murderer. Since he effectively destroys other human beings without regard to the lifelong suffering he inflicts, he should be treated in kind. Some people have gone so far as to advocate the death penalty for his likes. Jail sentences are no deterrent to the dope pusher since the "trade" is so profitable, and it is an anomaly of human nature that greed outstrips caution. There also may be some question as to the death sentence as a deterrent, but one thing is sure: Capital punishment spells finis to the mass-murder career of the particular offender.

Many methods heretofore used to cut crime have been gross failures. Efforts at rehabilitation have been perhaps one of the grossest. Since the "experts" have failed at reforming the criminal and turning him into a useful, law-abiding citizen, this writer can hardly spout expertise in this regard (although the ordinary citizen's "expertise" is probably as good as that of the "experts"). I would venture the thought, however, that prisoners should be taught trades, as some presently are, and fitted to be reintegrated into society. Further, their parole should include a period, possibly a year or more, of closely supervised gainful employment. Government-supported crime insurance could insure industry against losses if it undertook, at the behest of parole boards, to trust a convict who eventually returned to his former pursuits and bilked his employer.

On the other hand, governments themselves, if it should become necessary, might provide jobs for paroled convicts, such as road-building, etc., until the parolees showed themselves sufficiently re-habilitated to rejoin society.

In the past, some odd and some rather drastic measures were used in this country in attempts to repress the criminal. In 1933 then New York City Police Commissioner Edward Mulrooney advocated 30 to 40 lashes at the time the criminal entered prison, with others to be administered every half year thereafter. Vagrancy laws and "public enemy" laws were enacted in various states, as was a New Jersey law making being a "gangster" a felony punishable by 20 years imprisonment. The New Jersey law was struck down as unconstitutional by the U. S. Supreme Court.

As in "merrie old England," we could lop off hands and ears and an occasional nose or two as a deterrent to crime. But the American people like to believe that they're more civilized than were the denizens of England in that bygone day.

Still, in the wake of the raping of the 16-year-old girl in the Merrick, New York, church, a New York State legislator promptly called for the mandatory castration of men convicted of rape.

On the other end of the spectrum you have proposals to be more humane in the apprehension of suspects, even murderers, and in the recapturing of escaping criminals. One New York Congressman suggests the use of knockout pellets in police guns to immobilize suspects or escaping criminals without killing them. The weakness of the proposal is threefold: There is no nonlethal weapon presently available to replace the handgun; the difference between a lethal and nonlethal dosage of a knockout drug in pellet form is often so slight as to lead to guesswork; and while the knockout drug or tranquilizer is taking effect, a suspect not bound by the same rules could easily shoot a policeman dead.

Unquestionably, as many authorities speaking to the subject have pointed out, we need more policemen, policemen better trained, better equipped, better paid, and better supported by an informed public. As already indicated, the civic-minded, crime-hating citizen can be the eyes and ears of the policeman and report, with oftentimes telling effect, the slightest sign of crime in his area.

Too, communication methods should be improved. Even the foot patrolman should have a walkie-talkie or other two-way lightweight device to give him instantaneous communication with the precinct or with other members of the force.

In all, there are about 420,000 policemen attached to 40,000 separate agencies in the United States. The agencies spend about $2.5 billion a year in carrying out police work. It has been estimated that about two-thirds of the police forces of medium-size and large cities are below authorized strength. On a nationwide basis, cities themselves are about 10 percent below strength. Again on a national basis, in early 1967 about 50,000 additional policemen were needed the country round. Difficulties in recruitment plus the toughness of tests police candidates are required to pass make speedy recruitment of that number extremely difficult. Add to that the general apathy of the greater part of the public toward policemen and their work, low morale among already appointed policemen generated by civilian review board drives, and another telling factor, low pay in many areas, and you have some of the many reasons prospective candidates for police departments don't regard law enforcement careers as too attractive today.

Still, the non-policemen, the ordinary citizens who believe that the cancer called crime can only be cut out of the bowels of this nation by an aroused, alert, understanding, and helpful public standing shoulder to shoulder with the men behind the badge, can change all that. They can change it as some of the citizens of diverse places like Chicago, Indianapolis, and Wauwatosa, Wisconsin, have in their cities. They can report the slightest evidence of crime to policemen, making the apprehension of those engaged in criminal activity swifter, more certain, more effective.

That is, after all, the most important way to combat crime in America: the self-deputizing of every able-bodied citizen in this land to actively support *their* police in the everlasting crusade against crime.

When you see a loiterer acting suspiciously, pick up a phone and report the matter to the police.

When you spot a motorist speeding away from the scene of an accident, jot down his license number if you have time and report it quickly to the police.

In many states it is a misdemeanor to refuse to assist a law officer in arresting another person or in re-taking any person who has escaped from legal custody. But why should laws like these have to be invoked to place a citizen where he rightfully belongs, on the side of law and order? In the holy crusade against the unholy monster in our midst, we, one and all, should be willing and ready to help *our* police do battle to make America relatively safe once again from crime and criminals.

CHAPTER NINE

The Negro Revolution

IF AMERICA has learned anything at all from what has been styled by such stalwarts as deposed Congressman Adam Clayton Powell and others as the "Negro revolution" or the "black revolution," which tore at the vitals of many American cities during the hot summer of 1967, it has learned—or at least it should have learned—two inescapable lessons:

(1) That what begins as a relatively minor rock-throwing, bottle-tossing disturbance can flame into a major riot or virtual insurrection unless swift, forceful, decisive action is taken *right at the inception* of the disturbance to stifle it before it can possibly get out of hand.

(2) That there will be other "hot summers" with their outbreaks of racial violence, which some Washington, D. C. experts have gloomily predicted may last another 40 or 50 years, unless what are tantamount to "war plans" are adopted by all American cities and other political subdivisions which have large mixed populations, providing for an instantaneous show of overwhelming force and a grim, unwavering determination to use it against all lawless elements whose preachments of hate and violence have caused the killing of scores of Americans and the sacking of large urban areas.

A comparison of what happened in the summer of 1967 in four American cities—rather than a comparison, it is more appropriately a study in contrasts—proves the point.

Twenty-seven living souls, including at least one policeman and a fire captain felled by sniper-asassin bullets, died in Newark during five July days of rioting. In all, over 1200 persons were injured and some 1275 arrested as losses in burned out and destroyed property were put at $15 million.

Yet, Newark need not have happened. Twenty-seven persons need not have died. Scores of people need not have been made homeless, and businesses need not have been burnd to ashes.

None of this needed to have happened in Newark, New Jersey. And all of it could have been prevented if the forces of law and order on hand, the local police, had smashed what was described as a "protest" against police brutality on the first night the riotous conduct manifested itself, the night of July 12 and early morning of July 13, when a lawless Negro mob showed its utter contempt for law and order by hurling stones and Molotov cocktails at a Newark police stationhouse.

Now, admittedly, at this point there is some little doubt about who was telling the truth—Newark policeman Leonard F. Kowalewski, President of the New Jersey Lodge of the Fraternal Order of Police, or Newark Mayor Hugh J. Addonizio.

Kowalewski testified before the U. S. Senate Judiciary Committee probing the rash of riots in 1967, in answer to a question put by Senator John McClellan, that the Newark police were under "unofficial orders"—not written, but oral—to make no arrests when the rioting first erupted.

Senator McClellan went on to say: "In other words, there is no enforcement of the law? Law enforcement has broken down? These elements that are preaching the destruction of our cities and rioting . . . are the ones today who have immunity from law enforcement, is that correct?"

Officer Kowalewski answered: "That is absolutely correct. It is my opinion that the police across this entire nation have been more or less brainwashed into states of inactivity (so) that they are reluctant to do their job because any time it seems that they make an arrest, it is either a prelude or the beginning of a riot, the beginning of a sacking and looting of a city, or it's the beginning of some type of racial demonstration that goes beyond control. Again, it is my honest opinion that unless politics are taken out of the police department and the police profession, we will have these conditions from here on in, and God knows when they are going to stop."

Mayor Addonizio scoffed at Kowalewski's charge about hands-off instructions to the police and called it "nonsense."

Both gentlemen did agree on one rather salient point, however: that workers employed by an anti-poverty agency funded by the U. S. Office of Economic Opportunity had helped bring about the Newark rioting.

These assertions were bolstered by other police officers interviewed by a reporter for a television station. The policemen said they had been witnesses to inflammatory speeches made by persons receiving funds from the Office of Economic Opportunity. Offered was documentary evidence, in the form of pictures and handbills, distributed, it was said, by members of the Newark OEO.

Whether the Senate Judiciary Committee, a grand jury, or any other official body ever gets at the truth of what happened in Newark, New Jersey, in July, 1967, one fact is crystal clear: The time lag between inaction and action by the Newark police gives complete believability to officer Kowalewski's testimony.

On that fateful evening of July 12 and early morning of July 13, whether under the mayor's or anybody else's orders, the Newark police exercised remarkable restraint. They stayed in the stationhouse while an unruly mob pelted the place with stones and threw firebombs at it, showing that they could break the law with impunity in the environs of Newark. In fact, it was not until the night of July 13, when Negroes again tossed bottles and stones at the stationhouse for a full ten minutes, that the white-helmeted policemen sallied forth and drove the crowd back into a nearby housing project. By that time a volley of rocks had shattered 14 of the 25 front windows of the police station.

And so it was that a minor incident could have been nipped in the bud if the police had been permitted to carry out their main duty: to uphold the law of the land. It could have been done quickly, decisively, uncompromisingly. But no. The tiny spark, fueled by the arrest of a Negro taxicab driver allegedly the victim of police brutality—the excuse used; not the real reason for the rioting—touched off a major fire. And before the fire was snuffed out, a minor incident became a "criminal insurrection," in the words of New Jersey Governor Richard H. Hughes, who had to call out the National Guard to help state and city police quell the rioting.

In the interval, during which business and residential buildings blazed while police rode shotgun on fire trucks in efforts to protect firemen from snipers, one report had it that law and order had broken down to such an extent that Negro women were looting a supermarket in "leisurely fashion."

Whether City Hall had issued hands-off orders to the police or not, one thing is indisputable: There were many signs of impending trouble as much as a month or more before the rioting, which Mayor Addonizio and his administration had failed to properly assess. While trying to mollify, to some extent, the critics of the city, the administration should have nevertheless been preparing to defeat the forces of lawlessness if the worst should happen, as it did happen, in Newark, New Jersey. They were on notice, and they failed to act wisely, speedily, and effectively.

What I write here may be called an exercise in hindsight. But I shall presently demonstrate that it is no such thing.

As went Newark, so went Detroit.

Here, 43 persons died and somewhere between $250 and $500 millions of property was damaged or destroyed in an orgy of looting, firebombing, and shooting that could have been prevented—again, if the police had been under orders to take prompt, efficient, and effective action right at the beginning of what blossomed into a temporarily uncontrollable riot.

If, as in Newark, a "Roman holiday" atmosphere prevailed in Detroit, it was engendered, at least in part, by the restraint the police had apparently been ordered to exercise during the initial outbreak of disorder and violence.

Among the severe critics of the Detroit police for their failure to smother the disorders before they mushroomed into a full-blown riot was Longworth Quinn, editor of the Michigan CHRONICLE, the city's Negro newspaper. Quinn, with other Negro leaders, insisted that the looting on 12th Street, where the stealing started, would not have spread if it had been stopped quickly. Instead, the critics charged, the police allowed the looting to take on the form and substance of a "Roman holiday."

At one store, it was reported, when a lone police car appeared at about 4 A.M. Sunday, July 23, "50 kids piled out of the store." But when the Negroes saw the police were not going to stop them, the mobs swelled in size and the burning and looting intensified. One outspoken critic told a reporter that if the police had "started shooting the first few hours, it wouldn't have lasted a day."

But the carnival atmosphere spread as the lawless elements realized the police were not cracking down. And Negro homes and stores, along with those of the whites, were not necessarily spared. As a Negro leader charged that the lives of Negroes themselves were being "endangered by Negroes," one report had it that a Negro drugstore owner hefted a pistol as he supervised repairs to his heavily damaged store.

That Federal troops had to be called in to help the police and the National Guard put down the rioting simply demonstrates that the cost in lives and property of initial inaction can be frightful indeed

A study of what happened in Milwaukee, Wisconsin, when rioting broke out at the end of July presents a sharp contrast between political sagacity and political boobery.

Unlike other American cities, Milwaukee had a plan, devised 15 months before, to stop a riot right in its ugly, death-dealing, property-damaging tracks when and if it should erupt in that city.

And erupt it did in the waning hours of July. At one point roving bands of Negroes set fires and looted stores, shattered windows, and took potshots at police until a rainstorm forced them to scurry for cover.

After the initial stages of the rioting, two persons, one policeman and an elderly woman, had been killed; 100 persons had been injured, including 12 policemen, 7 of whom had been shot, and a fireman; and 275 persons had been arrested.

But Henry Maier, Mayor of Milwaukee, took the speedy, decisive action called for under the plan. He proclaimed a state of emergency, called for the National Guard within hours after the outbreak of violence, stoutly announced that there would be "no coddling of criminals, no excusing of criminal acts," and—this is the most important, most singular fact—imposed a 24-hour curfew as 4800 National Guardsmen were rushed in.

The stratagem worked. Life in a city of 750,000 souls abruptly ground to a halt. The rioting was effectively choked off before it could get out of hand. Only doctors and nurses and persons on emergency business were permitted to move in and about the streets of Milwaukee. Any unidentified persons found on the streets were subject to riot-control treatment. Hecklers and sightseers, often the victims of stray bullets when police and snipers shoot it out, were kept indoors. The sale of gasoline, ammunition, and liquor was banned throughout the city; and all looting reports were checked into immediately. And with every unauthorized person off the streets, there was much less chance of outbreaks of violence and disorder in lightly patrolled or even unpatrolled sections of the city.

Mayor Maier described the curfew as a "good, immediate cooling-off device."

It was, for it established the equivalent of martial law and stopped a riot smack in its criminal tracks.

Just how effective the technique was is pointed up by the fact that four rented armored Brink's trucks manned by police sharpshooters ready to pop away at snipers from protected portholes were practically not needed.

And while the second night of rioting in other cities had been generally worse, Milwaukee's second night was calmer than the first —so much so, in fact, that Mayor Maier re-imposed a 7 P.M. to daylight curfew.

Toledo is another American city whose handling of rioting right at the beginning demonstrated that swift, decisive action by the police and local administration is what is called for.

On Monday, July 24, Toledo was hit by a smattering of looting, firebombings, and rock tossings in Negro neighborhoods. A 9 P.M. curfew was imposed by the mayor on juveniles, the main perpetrators of the lawlessness. The National Guard was promptly called for, and reinforced police manned street barricades. Stores and taverns were closed, and armed guards were stationed outside, inside, and on the roofs of businesses jeopardized by the disturbances. The National Guard remained on standby duty at the local armory, though it had widely publicized orders to kill, if necessary, to maintain order. Meantime, the state police closely watched the half-mile stretch between the Ohio-Michigan state line to tip off the Toledo police if any automobiles with Michigan license plates tore south from Detroit.

The result: No deaths, not many injuries, and none of the major destruction of property that was so starkly evident in Newark and Detroit.

Toledo Mayor John W. Potter reportedly said in an interview: "The show of force tempered it into a rock-throwing contest.

"The Detroit situation had much to do with starting it. It was young people who felt they wanted to get into the act. They saw on television how Detroit police just monitored, without stopping, looting."

Of course, let it be added that the Toledo administration has done some effective race-relations work. It was largely instrumental in the recent passage of a strong fair-housing ordinance. And it has a Board of Community Relations whose executive director is a Negro, G. Nelson Smith. Mr. Smith, who met with some of the youths who took part in the violence, teaches a course for the police on minority relations.

There can be no dispute that where the police are not hamstrung by armchair politicians at city halls, whose worries about vote-garnering may outweigh any sense of duty that might impel them to make a firm stand for law and order, incidents of disorderliness or just plain lawlessness can be snuffed out before they grow into death-dealing riots.

In a way, what has happened in our cities has its parallel in Vietnam. There, where our soldiers are not permitted to fight an all-out war calculated to win with the least loss of Americans, American boys in the thousands are losing their lives. It is a war of containment that does not contain and certainly does not *attain*.

It is little different in our cities. Every year in the indefinite future may provide its own "hot summer" unless we strive to *attain* rather than to contain. As World War II and the Vietnam War have shown, guerilla warfare is a very effective means of destroying the enemy; and nobody knows better than the militant Negro with his "get whitey" battle cry just how effective this type of warfare can be in riot-torn, crime-ridden America.

Naturally, postmortems were not lacking in the wake of the disastrous riots of 1967. President Lyndon B. Johnson took the politician's standard out: He appointed a committee to "study" the situation. Investigations have been initiated by Congress, and a flood of "why it happened" reports will be forthcoming.

Who is responsible for rioting in American cities? The tendency on the part of what is regarded as the liberal American is to always blame society for all the ills that befall its citizens. Blame society, they say; never blame the criminal for the crime.

There can be slight question that the whole civil rights movement is basically responsible for what America is confronted with today. As Negro author and newspaperman George S. Schuyler has written (in an article copyrighted in 1967 by the North American Newspaper Alliance, Inc.):

"Race war is here, perhaps to stay; and while this will be denied, Negro leadership itself—including the so-called 'Moderates'—must share much of the blame for the smoking cities, the vandalism, and the armed attacks by some young Negroes on the forces of law and order."

There can equally be no question that the agitation for "civil rights" has given way to a campaign in which civil wrongs are committed in the name of civil rights. The demonstration has been replaced by the "demonstruction," as it were.

Add the "soft" approach of Dr. Martin Luther King, winner of the Nobel Peace Prize (showing that if one instigates enough civil strife, his peace-making propensities are bound to come to official notice), to the "hard" approach of Stokely Carmichael, former head of the Student Non-Violent Coordinating Committee (as fine a piece of semantic trickery as anyone could invent), and of H. Rap Brown, new leader of SNCC, and you have all the excuse needed for the riots that have ripped American cities. Just what part the Communist Party played in the instigation of the riots remains to be disclosed by Congressional committees probing that phase of the situation, but that they played a part can hardly be controverted, for the Communist Party historically feeds upon social unrest.

At any rate, when H. Rap Brown calls upon his militant followers to burn down Washington, D. C.; to loot gun stores especially; not to "love the white man to death; shoot him to death;" and when the school dropouts and criminal elements in a given area respond dramatically by doing just that, what are the law-abiding Negro and white citizens to assume if not that the black power advocates such as Brown and Carmichael want to take over the U. S. Government by force and violence?

And when Carmichael visits Communist Cuba and Hanoi in defiance of our laws and tells mobs of cheering Castroites that the American Negroes are organizing urban guerillas for a "fight to the death," precisely what are the law-abiding majority of Americans to conclude from these death threats delivered by a preacher of "non-violence"?

On the other hand, other remarks of Brown are a study in twisted reasoning that almost defies comparison. He told a group of Negroes that whites have embarked on a "conspiracy of genocide" and pointed to the Vietnam conflict to support his charge. There, he claimed, 30 percent of the casualties are Negro soldiers, who are thereby the victims of the white conspiracy to "exterminate Negroes."

It makes real sense, of course, to "conspire" to kill off 70 whites out of each 100 persons to "get" 30 Negroes out of each 100 Americans engaged in the Vietnam fighting.

The pity of all this is that the black power advocates cannot see the peril of their own position. The term "race riot," as applied to the recent wave of riots, is a misnomer. "Race riot" implies conflict between races, white and black in this case. Actually, the white population has as yet taken no active part in the rioting. It has allowed the police, the National Guard, and Federal troops to handle the "revolution." But that isn't to say that the "kill whitey" preachers of hate couldn't actually incite a full-blown, real, honest-to-God race riot.

The mayor of San Bernardino, California, for example, has urged the citizens of his city to arm themselves to protect their own property, not to say their lives. He also urged city firemen to carry rifles on fire trucks to guard against interference by snipers when responding to fire alarms. Next, he gave instructions to the police that anyone throwing rocks, bottles, or Molotov cocktails was "to be shot."

As a result of the mayor's call to arms, the sale of guns skyrocketed and the police were swamped with applications for gun permits. Up to this writing, San Bernardino has been an extremely quiet city.

Let us all pray that a real race war never comes to pass in this nation that is so free that a man can publicly call for the murder of other citizens because of the color of their skin and get away with it; for the badly outnumbered Negro would suffer mightily at the hands of an enraged white population in such an event.

Besides, the majority of American Negroes are peaceful, law-abiding citizens. It is largely some Negro youths, including school dropouts, and Negroes with prior criminal records that constitute the minority of Negroes who respond to cries to burn down our cities, to "kill whitey," and to steal anything they can get their hands on, but guns especially. New Jersey Governor Richard Hughes, for instance, has pointed out that the holocaust in Newark was brought about by under five percent of its Negroes. Of that five percent, the Governor added significantly, more than half had criminal records.

Nobody really knows how many guns have been sold to whites and Negroes since the riots erupted. But the number is substantial; and the whites, besides their superiority in numbers, concededly have the greater purchasing power.

Beyond calling for black universities, some of the black power advocates who assert their superiority over whites and call not for integration, but segregation, also would like a black state of their own. It would be an interesting social experiment to give it to them. Why not relocate the Indians now occupying a couple of large Indian reservations and let the black powermen settle the area—on a voluntary basis, of course. With the help of the Federal Government (after the 1967 riots, two U. S. senators wanted to pump another billion into the riot ghettos to cool them off), a "nation within a nation" could be built up; and the black power proponents could have their own housing, their industry, their own cities, and their own forms of government.

I am inclined to believe that not too many Negroes would volunteer to settle such an area. Still, it would be interesting, highly revelatory even, to see just what would happen should the black powermen be given the independence they claim to crave.

The 1967 riots taught us much. They taught us that some police and National Guard units don't know enough about coping with the sniper, that deadly assassin who's not brave enough or perhaps not stupid enough to face his victim. The Guard was criticized in some places for shooting too much; in others, for not shooting enough. And the police, the embattled police who must bear the brunt of all massive public attacks on law and order, had the usual charges of brutality hurled at them after they had helped put down the "revolution."

The riots also have spotlighted the effectiveness of helicopters in the anti-crime war. Using huge searchlights, the choppers can, as some of them have, fly over rooftops and flood them with light, exposing any sneaky sniper who may be lurking there. Parenthetically, in Lakewood, California, a year-long experiment in using helicopters in round-the-clock patrols is still underway. Films of the operations have shown that the choppers are, rather miraculously, just as effective at night as they are in daylight. The telecast films showed that motorcycle gangs which tear up a town and then cycle their way to freedom can't escape the 'copter, which can radio the police below the exact location of the cyclists and make their apprehension almost routine. The films also depicted the catching of a hit-and-run driver who was escaping the ground police, but could not escape the chopper. They demonstrated too the value of the helicopter in uncovering vandalism in process; in bathing a prowler in light, scaring him off; and even during an accident at night, when light from the air helped untangle tied-up traffic.

The lessons taught by the riots have triggered action in some quarters. New York City, perhaps acting on recommendation of the FBI, which advocates sharpshooter anti-sniper teams to minimize loss of life, particularly among innocent bystanders in riot areas, has set up special anti-sniper teams equipped with binoculars, telescopic sights and high-powered rifles. Also in August, 1967, it began experiments with a tear-gas spray designed to reduce a would-be police battler to tears at 20 paces. The spray, said to be harmless, is claimed to be "extremely effective" in subduing a deranged individual or a hoodlum bent on attacking the police.

Since the riots, National Guardsmen are being given riot-control training, including, no doubt, some anti-sniper training similar to that used by Marines in Vietnam, which has now been adopted by the New York City Police.

In Chapter 10 I propose the equivalent of a national police force, cooperatively run by the Federal and state governments to cope with all forms of crime, including rioting, so there is no need to dwell upon it here.

The astounding attitude of many rioters during the 1967 looting and burning sprees anent the part they played in the lawlessness is worthy of mention. One woman queried on the radio about looting in Newark defended the stealing by saying: "The people only took what they needed. They didn't take anything they didn't need."

Others saw little, if anything, wrong with what they termed "self-service shopping." They argued that white storekeepers had been robbing the Negroes for years anyway through ultra-high prices and said they were merely getting back at "whitey."

A man who readily admitted taking part in the rioting said: "I went out Thursday night rioting, you know, looting, doing everything. On Friday . . . I did the same thing, stole everything I could get my hands on." He added that if he had had a gun, he would have shot a white man and "thought nothing about it."

In discussing Negro attitudes, the rat-control bill voted down by the House of Representatives in the summer of 1967 also deserves a word. Negro leaders have made much of the fact that the House at first refused to provide $40 million to fight rats on a local basis. The criticism waxed so hot, in fact, that the House was accused of even thinking more of rats than it does of human beings. The result: In September, 1967, the House made a complete turnabout and okayed a two-year, $40 million rat-control program.

It is hard to convince an old farm boy like me that if people seriously want to destroy rats they need the might and power, not to say money, of that Big Father figure, the Federal Government, behind them.

When we found our barn overrun with rats, we merely spread rat poison all about and soon exterminated just about the entire rat population in the immediate vicinity. Admittedly, more sophisticated methods might have to be used in crowded cities because of the danger of poisoning children. But here is one citizen who cannot see why local departments of health and the citizens themselves, working cooperatively and jointly, can't rid a given area of rats.

There are many ways to wipe out the rodent. Traps are only too obvious. Cats, preferably of the alley variety—not the spoiled purebreds who are rarely permitted off the living room sofa—are instinctive enemies of both rats and mice and are prime rodent slayers.

Of course, New York Governor Nelson Rockefeller emerged as a rat-fighting hero in that state after the Congressional defeat of the national rat-control bill. He got the state to undertake a $4.5 million program to exterminate rats, including a sterilization program aimed at making the dirty rats highly unfertile.

In the case of New York City, as a prime example as a rat haven, one wonders where the New York State and City Health Departments have been down through the years when rats were propagating prodigiously in slums and posing a constant threat to the human population.

When one reads about all the agitation by Negro leaders for a Federal rat-control bill, he wonders, too, about the resourcefulness of the American Negro. And he harkens to the words of the late author, William Faulkner, who said in a letter to his one-time Negro butler that neither the police nor military bayonets could give the Negroes the equality they seek.

In pointing out that Negroes must earn their equality, he wrote:

"As I see it, if the people of your race are to have equality and justice as human beings in our culture, the majority of them have got to be changed completely from the way they now act. Since they are a minority, they must behave better than white people. They must be more responsible, more honest, more moral, more industrious, more literate and educated. They, not the law, have got to compel the white people to say, Please come and be equal with us. If the individual Negro does not do this by getting himself educated and trained in responsibility and morality, there will be more and more trouble between the two races."

Instead of adopting "kill whitey" war cries at the behest of Communists and black power extremists, the Negro (and I by no means wish to imply that all Negroes fall into this classification) should adopt a "kill rats" war cry. And I am sure that "whitey," right at his doorstep, not "whitey" in Washington, D. C., will help the Negro do precisely that, once he sees that the Negro is making at least an attempt to help himself.

To take up a less emotional, but exceedingly more important issue, I think I have sufficiently discussed in other chapters the immorality of any man, no matter what his color, being unemployed in this land of plenty. Employment insurance, rather than unemployment insurance, and amendments to child-labor laws to provide jobs for youths as young as 14, or even younger, would go a long way toward creating total employment. If not, such efforts could be supplemented by others. The working youth who has won dignity and self-respect through the sweat of his brow is hardly likely to be tossing Molotov cocktails at "whitey."

Assuredly, not money alone should be pumped into ghettos; rather, I would pump opportunity into them, opportunity to work, to be "more honest, more responsible, more moral, more industrious, more literate and educated," as the late Mr. Faulkner so aptly put it.

Fight rats? Surely, but let's fight all forms of immorality. The white man and the Negro could best do that by working together, not by using each other as choice targets.

It is hard to imagine how ghetto problems can be permanently solved without a planned depopulation of the ghettos and a dispersal of the Negro throughout the land—a manifest impossibility, overnight at least, for economic and other reasons. (The poor white man, for example, can't move into a rich white neighborhood simply because he can't afford it.)

But the Negro deserves a place in the sun. If he strives for it, he will earn it. If he shows respect, not disrespect, for the forces of law and order in this land, he will be treated equally respectfully. Just as hate breeds hate, so too does respect engender respect.

During the heat of the riots of 1967, I walked among many Negroes in the area in which I live. It has a large Negro population, some of whose families undoubtedly have lived there since the days of the American Revolution. These people are respected members of the community. There was no trouble, for I believe there is an unspoken bond of mutual respect between us. I didn't question any of them about the matter, but I firmly believe that many of these respected members of our community were truly aghast at the "kill whitey" cries echoing and re-echoing in other parts of the United States.

These people are respected (not all of them are middle-class Negroes either) because they have earned the respect of which Mr. Faulkner so eloquently wrote.

CHAPTER TEN

Antidote for the Poison of Crime

IS THERE ANY SINGLE, overall antidote for the poison of crime which courses through the lifestream of this country?

There is. Simply put, to neutralize the virulence called crime there must be a rebirth of honesty, a reinfusion of morality in our nation. Only a people who are themselves moral, upright, unshakably honest can hope to cope with and eradicate crime. If we don't eradicate it, in time it will eradicate us. The threat is that simple.

To a good extent, money is the only god universally recognized today; materialism, the only religion. True, there is greater attendance of churches nowadays, possibly even a greater proportionate attendance. Nevertheless, there is less faith. Religion has been steadily losing ground, and the moral precepts it teaches and espouses have been cast out of our houses and out of our hearts.

More, those who worship at the shrine of materialism have other gods. Science, or what sometimes masquerades as science, is one of them. In it, the people have found themselves a new god just as unknowable really, just as untouchable, just as unobservable as the true God, but a god more to their liking, for the god of science holds the promise of Utopia, the man-made, science-sponsored heaven on earth in which machines, the handtools of science, will give to man the ultimate life of ease, of indolence, of sloth which he equates with heaven. And it is not a *hereafter heaven,* but a *now heaven,* now, right here on earth.

It follows that once the religion of our fathers grows weaker, less influential in its preachments that good must be placed above evil and that the man who desires immorality must be at peace both with his God and with himself, there is a natural erosion and corrosion of family life, a general disintegration of the moral fabric which should bind a family together. And when the family dies, so dies the nation.

103

Harrisburg, Pennsylvania, attorney Genevieve Blatt, a member of the Pennsylvania State Board of Pardons from 1955 to 1967 (to date) and a member of the President's Crime Commission, took rather sharp issue with her fellow commissioners for their failure in the 340-page Commission report to "recognize godlessness as a basic cause of crime and religion as a basic cure."

Miss Blatt's words are so significant that they merit quotation in full. She said:

"Thorough as the Commission's studies have been and comprehensive as its valuable recommendations are, its report seems deficient to me in that it neglects to recognize godlessness as a basic cause of crime and religion as a basic cure.

"The report acknowledges the necessity for activating religious institutions in the war on crime, and it mentions some of the excellent work religious groups have done in youth work and along similar lines.

"But nowhere does the report mention the Ten Commandments which underlie our Judaeo-Christian culture. Nor does it mention the God who created all of us, who gave us the Ten Commandments, who enforces a law higher than ours and who administers the ultimate justice.

"Admittedly, it would not be within the province of the Commission to recommend how to combat the godlessness so prevalent today and so basically at the root of so much of our crime problem. Nor could the Commission properly outline how religion, as a moral force distinct from an institutional group, could help control crime.

"But just as the report recognizes the obvious relationship of poverty and ignorance and discrimination to an increasing crime rate, it should recognize that man's alienation from his God has also been a crime-inducing factor.

"It is true that the all too frequent unwillingness of many religious groups and of many presumably religious individuals to live by and not just to profess the moral precepts common to all religions has all too frequently blunted the effectiveness of religion in preventing crime. Nevertheless, properly used, religion is a real weapon. And it should be used.

"My feeling is that we unquestionably should, as the Commission suggests, improve family life and the school system and every other human institution. In so doing we will undoubtedly help prevent crime.

"To do these things, however, without renewing and revitalizing religious life, won't be enough.

"Somehow or other we must restore to every citizen's everyday living that same belief in God's love and justice which was characteristic of our countrymen in an earlier and less crime-ridden period of our history.

"We were a God-fearing people at one time, and proud of it. We must be that again if we expect to see the crime rate substantially reduced."

What about the Ten Commandments? Are they actually passé today? Science doesn't say so, not in so many words at least (though there is that internationally known psychiatrist who claims that morality is a bar to good mental health).

No, the Decalogue is not really dead. The Ten Commandments, a concise statement of the divine law in Judaism, Christianity, and Islam, which have withstood the ravages of the ages, can similarly withstand direct or indirect gambits by science and secularism to dissipate our faith in Almighty God.

"Thou shalt have no other god besides me," says the First Commandment.

In a highly irreligious society, how is it possible to have only one God? Or any God at all, for that matter?

Or take Commandment Four: "Remember the Sabbath-day, to hallow it."

The Sabbath should be a day of rest, of peace, of communion with God. It is with the truly religious among us, but the bulk of the people are not truly religious. Mere church attendance is not necessarily an indication of deep and abiding faith.

Commandment Five: "Honor thy father and thy mother."

Children should be taught respect for their parents and for older folk in general from the cradle to adulthood. In the happy, well-knit family the teaching is never direct; it is only implied, but the lesson is powerful.

Juvenile delinquency is said to be practically nonexistent among the Chinese. Why? Because parents and other forebears are not just obeyed; they're revered.

On the other hand, this Commandment could conceivably have a few words added to it: "Parents, honor thy children." Those who *beget,* then *forget,* might well hearken to that sort of commandment.

Commandment Six: "Thou shalt not kill."

If universally observed, this Commandment would make war impossible. It would prevent the murder of as many as 6,934 persons in a single year (1965) in this country.

And it would have saved the life of a Nassau County, New York, police officer some years ago who was shotgunned into eternity by a young man who had tattooed on his chest in large letters: "I hate cops."

"Thou shalt not commit adultery," says Commandment Seven.

If this Commandment were strictly obeyed, there likely wouldn't be so many fatherless, motherless, and otherwise unwanted children in this world.

The courts are full of cases in which adulterers are brought to book, in a manner of speaking, for their trespasses against their God, if they believe in any, and against the children they summon into the world and then desert. Thus are the issue of their loins given unforgettable examples of the adult adultery kind of morality in America.

One civil law says a man cannot have a harem in the United States. But other civil laws and their manipulators say otherwise. A man can have as many wives as he chooses (or a woman as many husbands), provided he or she doesn't have them concurrently. So it is *concurrent*, not *consecutive*, harems that are taboo. It is just a matter of timing and of following irreligious and immoral laws to the letter.

"Thou shalt not steal."

So speaks Commandment Eight. I used to say—rather cynically —that the man who sticks a gun in your ribs and relieves you of your wallet is in a way to be respected: He's honestly a crook and doesn't pretend to be anything but.

But the subtle, indirect forms of stealing by persons who outwardly profess to be honest are something else again.

The politician or public official who takes graft—surreptitiously, of course—is guilty of a crime, but the guilt is hard to pin on him because transactions like that never take place in the open. The public official who places relatives and others on public payrolls, the main jobs of the payrollees being to transport their paychecks to the bank periodically, is similarly guilty of a subtle form of stealing, though the law generally imposes no sanctions on such men as it tacitly recognizes this practice as "legitimate."

The President's Crime Commission rightfully looks aghast at

corporate crime (which I prefer to call "white collar crime"), the enormity of which strains the imagination. Price fixing some years ago by 29 electrical companies, it points out, "probably cost utilities, and therefore, the public more money than is reported as stolen by burglars in a year."

Other types of crime can be even more injurious than those that hit one in the pocketbook. Tainted foods and harmful drugs sold in violation of the Pure Food and Drugs Act can cost one not money alone, but his life to boot.

The Commission admits that reducing the "scope of business crime" is extremely difficult. The offenses are often hard to uncover, it says, since there is no particular victim except the general public.

The public usually tends to countenance "white collar crime" that doesn't hit it directly in the pocketbook. Generally speaking, if a highly popular politician is caught with his hands in the public till and is convicted of stealing, once he's out of jail, if he serves a sentence at all, he's almost certain to be re-elected to office.

That doesn't speak well for the morality of the American public. Nor do crime cover-ups on the part of business speak well for the morality of the business community.

Once I attended a hearing inquiring into the activities of an insurance broker who collected dozens of premiums for policies, the proceeds of which he put in his own pocket and spent like a man who had suddenly come into a large inheritance. Was the insurance company interested in prosecuting the man? Hardly. It did no such thing, on the premise, presumably, that the prosecution of the agent for his defalcations would hurt the public image of the insurance company.

There is actually no way of determining how much in dollars and cents is the annual cost of property crimes in America. Pilferage on the part of light-fingered employees alone must run into the billions.

Nor are edifices like public buildings exempt from thievery. Some years ago, I noticed the huge Christmas tree in the Mineola, New York, Courthouse lobby was draped in semi-darkness.

"What, no Christmas tree lights this year?" I asked one of the maintenance men.

"No," he said sadly, "somebody swiped them."

"Oh, somebody lit out with the lights," I quipped.

We treated the matter *lightly;* yet it showed that even a courthouse is fair game for a thief.

Another maintenance man used to lock up his tube-type vacuum cleaner in one of my file cabinets as a safety measure. Just too many things had acquired the habit of disappearing from the courthouse annex.

When the maintenance man was succeeded by a newcomer, the latter asked me one day, "Where is the vacuum cleaner? I can't find it in the utility room or anywhere else."

"It's right here in that lower file cabinet drawer, locked up," I said. "I have a duplicate key which you may have. But I'd advise you to keep it locked up and not in the utility room either. There are too many duplicate keys in the building."

"There's no need for that," he scoffed. "I'll keep it downstairs. It'll be all right."

Two days later it joined its predecessors, another vacuum cleaner and a carpet sweeper, in "taking a walk" and disappearing forever.

These are minor crimes, not quite so important, perhaps, as the three brand-new electric typewriters that vanished from judges' chambers right after having been bolted down on desks. Yet, crimes like these should be of major concern to all of us. If courthouses aren't safe from crime and criminals, a citizen can well ask: Is anybody or anything safe any more?

In the spring of 1967 the homes of two policemen who had just died from natural causes were broken into on the day of their funerals. A few valuables were stolen, but the police theorized that the thieves weren't really after money or jewelry; they were looking for the dead policemen's guns.

"Thou shalt not bear false witness," the Ninth Commandment reads.

Mark Twain once said a diplomat is nothing but an international liar.

What are we to say about domestic governmenters who go so far as to invent a lying phrase like "credibility gap" to soften the impact of their prevarications?

That professionals of various stripes do endow themselves with the right to lie is a conclusion I arrived at during more than nine years of newspaper reporting.

During the pendency of litigation levelled at the East Meadow, New York, school board in 1960,* which had refused to show me my

---

* See *Van Allen v. McCleary*, 211 New York Supplement (2d) 501.

child's school record, a member of the school board announced at a public meeting (at which I, the father in question, was not present, naturally) that it had offered to exhibit the record to the parent. In point of fact, I at that very instant had in my possession a letter signed by the then president of the board in which it was stated that the board absolutely refused to show me the record.

During a teachers' campaign for higher pay, a group of teachers suddenly announced that they were going on a "sick strike." When they reached a rather fast settlement, they just as suddenly became "well" again. A newspaper which reported the settlement quite artfully headlined its story: "Teachers' Health Suddenly Improves."

The kind of example teachers who happen to be adults or are presumed to be adults set for children through little dishonesties like these needs no further treatment here.

In a country in which lying is believed by some to be a national pastime, it is difficult to pick particular forms of the "art" to discuss. Since I have had much to do with courts of law in which people hold up their hands and swear to "tell the truth, the whole truth, and nothing but the truth," perhaps I'll stick to a subject I know best.

Once I saw a court clerk swear in a witness preparatory to the latter's being examined before trial by two attorneys. As the trio turned to leave after the witness had been sworn, the court clerk said under his breath: "Now go on outside and lie like hell!" Experience does sometimes breed cynicism.

Again, as I was walking along a street, I heard a lawyer coaching his client. "If the other side asks you this question," he advised, "answer it this way . . . If he asks you this question, tell him this . . ."

At no time did I hear this attorney advise his client to tell the truth. On the contrary, the words the "officer of the court" was putting in his client's mouth were probably as far from the truth as the North Pole is from the South.

"Thou shalt not bear false witness." In the courts that Commandment might well be amended to add: "Unless you may find it very profitable to lie."

Jewish and Christian traditions have dictated slight differences in the cataloguing of the Ten Commandments. Most Protestant churches divide the Jewish Second Commandment into two, making the first sentence the First Commandment and the remainder the Second Commandment. The Roman Catholic and Lutheran Churches on the other hand, divide the Jewish Tenth Commandment into two, forming a new Ninth reading, "Thou shalt not covet thy neighbor's wife," and a Tenth, reading, "Thou shalt not covet thy neighbor's house, nor his manservant, nor his maidservant, nor his ox, nor his ass, nor anything that is thy neighbor's." The numerical sequence is changed initially, of course, by combining the first two Commandments into one.

In any event, whether the Tenth Commandment is considered as a unit or not, human greed would be no more were it faithfully abided by. The truly religious, genuinely moral man is not a jealous, avaricious person out to take anything that is not rightfully his. But such men and women are heavily in the minority.

Greed is so deeply ingrained in our culture, in our personalities, that few of us would take heed of this precept. Still, how many among us would be like the man who, with his own wife in the hospital, periodically stole across the back yard to the house next door to visit a female neighbor whose husband happened to be working nights? Or who among us, professional men included, does not turn to price-gouging when he's in the "driver's seat" and can charge for his goods or services whatever the traffic will bear?

Verily, some of us must believe that the walls of the kingdom of heaven are lined with greenbacks. We all have heard the expression, "You can't take it with you." Ah, but you can. Were it not that we might possibly cut off some inheritor direly in need, I would advocate that all the worldly worth of the fiercely greedy man be buried with him when he dies. That would be the final tribute to man's greed.

Why not the ageless Ten Commandments? Why couldn't we re-adopt them as a national code of ethics? The U. S. Supreme Court probably wouldn't permit the Commandments to be taught in school, even in courses like the History of Ethics. But parents could—and should—teach their children almost from the time of infancy the meaning of the law of God, as handed down to Moses. They should teach them to live by the Decalogue's eternal precepts. They should teach them, partially by setting good examples, the value of "old-fashioned" concepts like honesty, integrity, decency, goodwill of man toward man.

Governments too must set better standards for the governed to follow. There should be no heinous things like "credibility gaps" among governmenters. If national security makes release of a particular fact too risky for the nation, then the government should withhold that fact from the people, but honestly give national security as the reason for the refusal to release the information.

Governments, from the Congress on down, also should adopt stiff ethics codes. There is an ever-present, ever-evident need for more self-policing on the part of government. One reason for the lack of strong codes of conduct among legislative bodies is the fact that most legislators are lawyers whose efforts at amassing great personal wealth would be seriously hampered by strong ethics codes. (Take the legislator-lawyer prohibited from practicing before government agencies as an example.) Nonetheless, legislators are elected to office to repreesnt *all* the people, not to represent their own pocketbooks.

Long ago a man said, "Any government which operates on the spoils system is foundationally corrupt." It need not be. The spoils system should be abolished. Using public moneys for party payoffs to the faithful who helped elect a particular politician or members of a political party to office is an odiously immoral practice. Throughout the nation appointment via open competitive civil service examinations should replace appointment by political favor.

So too with judges. Those elected through the "good graces" of political parties should be selected in some other fashion.

Says the President's Crime Commission in its 340-page report:

"The elective process, particularly if judges are elected as candidates of political parties, has not proven an effective system for choosing persons to fill an office as removed from daily political pressures as the judiciary should be. Selection of candidates tends to be dictated to an excessive degree by party considerations . . . And the electoral process gives the voters little opportunity to weigh the relative abilities of the candidates. *** Judicial appointments should be made on grounds other than partisanship, and sitting judges should be free from political obligations."

That judges should be beyond reach, beyond so much as a suggestion that they might be tainted by politics goes without saying. This observer of the legal scene for more than a quarter century would favor special schools for the training of judges who had practiced as attorneys for perhaps five years beforehand, and very stiff examinations, both written and oral, to prove their qualifications, intellectually and temperamentally, for office before appointment, which would be for possibly ten years or more during good and efficient behavior.

If governments need stiff ethics codes, something additional is required to secure the people against breaches of the public trust. Needed are laws which would make the public officer who breaches the faith reposed in him by the people punishable on two counts: (1) for violating his public trust; and (2) for whatever other crime he may have committed in so violating his trust.

Breach-of-trust laws should apply with equal force to policemen. Law enforcement officers have temptations thrust at them every day of the week. A speeder offers a policeman a $20 bill to forget the matter. The honest officer arrests the man for attempted bribery. The dishonorable man puts the money in his pocket, and we then unknowingly have two dishonest men, the briber and the bribed.

Unfortunately, public officials sometimes are found to be "on the take." That is why the law should deal with them even more harshly than it does with the non-public official accused of a similar crime. While businessmen and other private citizens may accept Christmas or other presents for favors performed or services rendered, public officers must not. It is commensurately unfortunate that rules and regulations aimed at curbing the taking of graft or what is tantamount to graft don't stamp out the practice completely. They just insure surreptitiousness on the part of the taker and the "taken."

In any discussion of crime and corruption in government, the words of the late Louis Brandeis, Associate Justice of the U. S. Supreme Court (1916-1939), are arresting. He said:

"Decency, security and liberty alike demand that government officials shall be subjected to the same rules of conduct that are commands to the citizen. In a government of laws, existence of the government will be imperiled if it fails to observe the law scrupulously. Our government is the potent, the omnipresent teacher. For good or for ill, it teaches the whole people by its example. Crime is contagious. If the government becomes a law-breaker, it breeds contempt for law; it invites every man to become a law unto himself; it invites anarchy."

If national, state, and local governments and professional people in various walks of life should be exemplary models of integrity based on the premise that we cannot expect our children to be any more honest, any more decent, any more upright than their elders, religion itself must be revitalized as a moral force in America. The respective religions might well embark on drives to bring the word of God into every home in the country, at the same time attempting to bring not single individuals, but whole families into the fold.

The child who has the virtues of honesty and goodness instilled in him when very young is not likely to be a law-breaker at 10 or 15 or 25. More, the child taught to love and worship God and His teachings is not apt to grow up into a neurotic, unhappy soul who bounces from marriage to marriage and, worst of all, will never in his lifetime understand precisely why he acts as he does.

True, church attendance is not, by itself, evidence of real faith. Yet, if huge numbers of adults are beyond redemption in many ways, children are not. On the contrary, they will be better citizens, the nation itself will be better if the moral law enunciated by the Ten Commandments is made part of the pattern of their lives from the time they are old enough to understand what the words signify.

In Chicago, which has been the scene of teenage gang violence and repeated instances of theft, assault, robbery, and other crimes, conditions got so bad in March, 1967, that teachers in two schools threatened to go on strike unless the police provided greater protection. Similarly frightened neighborhood groups of mothers formed emergency escort brigades to protect children going to and from school.

For their part, police complained that Illinois laws have hampered them in cracking down on the disruptive, disorderly, and crime-prone youths. Citizens, on the other hand, took enforcement of the law into their own hands to some extent by forming vigilante groups as a means of neighborhood protection.

One wonders how gangs of hoodlums like these could possibly spring up, even in disadvantaged, underprivileged, or deprived areas, if the insecure individuals who join gangs had proper beginnings: good families who reared them in a religious, hence moral environment.

Has anyone ever heard of the truly religious youth or adult joining a gang? Or of any sincerely religious person stealing so much as a farthing from a fellow citizen?

There are other conditions in this nation which bespeak immorality and cry out for correction. The squalor and poverty one descries in rat-infested slums are essentially immoral in a land that rightfully boasts of plenty because it produces plenty. It is likewise many times more immoral for the state to keep a family on welfare for a lifetime because it finds it easier to do that than to cope with and solve such "monumental" problems as getting able-bodied men and women jobs through and by which they can regain their sense of personal worth callously taken from them by government with its demeaning welfare programs.

Other areas of life in America which involve unethical rather than rankly unlawful conduct merit a mite of inquiry. Small-loan laws which permit as much as 36 percent interest despite the legal rate of 6 percent in a particular state demand reappraisal. Who pays the 36 percent? Those least able to afford it, the poor who must turn to small-loan companies because the banks consider them poor risks.

Practices of banks in this field could also stand a little probing. If a man borrows $800, let us say, from a bank at 6 percent interest, and the interest, $48, is deducted in advance so that he receives a net loan of only $752, then he is in reality paying $48 interest on a loan of $752. As anyone can see, the rate is higher than the legal 6 percent rate here referred to. Moreover, if he borrows the money for a year and has to pay it back periodically in the meantime, then he will, in the interim, be paying interest on money that's actually back in the possession of the bank. Such are two examples of the legerdemain practiced on paper by that sort of bank.

A judge who has since passed on to his reward used to call public-bilking practices sanctioned by one law despite other laws on the books which would otherwise prohibit them forms of "legal larceny."

A creative writer who wrote a book on his pet subject, creative writing, had this advice for budding authors devoid of ideas for articles or stories. (This is paraphrased; I've forgotten the source):

Is your mind barren of ideas for articles? Then look around you. You'll find that somebody's always rooking somebody else. And that, my friend, gives you an inexhaustible source for story ideas.

I know a man who insured his boat with a large insurance company. It was a brand-new boat, but at the end of the first year it had, like a car, depreciated considerably. When the company sent him a new policy, not a word did it say about depreciation. This person was worldly wise from a business standpoint. He knew, as many of us know, that if you suffer a total loss, insurance companies will not necessarily give you the amount the article is insured for, which means they've been overcharging you in the first place. They'll more likely give you what *they* declare to be its book value.

At any rate, the man sent both the policy and the bill for it back. "What about depreciation?" he scrawled across the face of the bill. In due time, the policy, an endorsement, and a new bill were remailed to the boat owner. The company agreed that the boat and its accessories had indeed depreciated, in this case by $1,555, for a total premium saving of $62 to the boat owner.

The next year, history repeated. Again a new boat policy came in the mail. And again no depreciation was allowed.

Once more the policy and bill were returned to the company. And once more it acknowledged having made a "mistake." It dropped the cost of the policy another $23.

When the "mistake" came through the third year, the boat owner wrote no more notes about depreciation. He simply canceled the policy, figuring a company with assets in the millions was just out to bilk him. He wondered, though, about how many hundreds of persons with similar boat policies paid exorbitant premiums on boats that had markedly depreciated in value.

Now he deals with an insurance company which depreciates his boat from year to year without any reminders from him.

If practices like these are not outrightly illegal, they certainly are downrightly unethical and don't exactly enhance the public image of any company practicing them.

The multivarious forms of immorality which taint life in America could easily be the subject of a separate book, a veritable tome. They are merely touched upon here to indicate the vastness of the problem that is the basic cause of crime in all its black varieties.

SUMMATION

Departing for the moment from the thesis that the people of the United States must, if they want to stop crime in its crooked tracks, cause the rebirth of morality, of decency, of respect for law and order, what about those forefront fighters against crime, our policemen, who receive so much attention when they are charged with wrongdoing and so little notice when they right the wrongs of others?

While we, the people, are busy upgrading ourselves morally and spiritually (and let us not deceive anyone, least of all ourselves: moral and spiritual re-armament in America as well as in the world at large is realizable only if enough people hunger for it sufficiently to bring it about), we must necessarily upgrade our front-line "soldiers" in the war against crime.

That war must be a total war, an all-out war. And if it is to be a winnable war, there should be, there must be a total effort, a total mobilization of all our human resources, all forces and agencies having to do with law enforcement, and a total realization by the people of this land that piecemeal, haphazard, ununified, sporadic thrusts against crime and the criminal don't amount to so much as a delaying action against an enemy which propagates faster than "crimicides" can be manufactured to destroy it.

That totality of effort means that every law-abiding citizen in this country must stand solidly behind our 420,000 policemen.

One approach might be the formation of a National Crime Bureau, in which the Federal and state governments would be co-equal partners, to root out and wipe out crime in every walk of life on a national scale. That kind of combined Federal-state setup could establish a national crime laboratory to use the latest scientific methods in attacking crime. It could exchange information with its members on the latest crime-fighting techniques. And most importantly, it could establish a national network of police-training schools whose aim would be the production of officers educated to the nth degree in ways of combating crime. These schools could award police science degrees similar to those now granted by some colleges.

If FBI training is superior to that given the average local policeman—and the best opinion appears to be that it is—then by all means let us have the equivalent of FBI training for all policemen throughout the nation.

Parenthetically, the FBI Police Academy in Washington, D. C. provides some direct training of police officers now. But the training effort is hardly the total effort required if we are to substantially wipe out crime in the United States.

Concededly, police forces, in our larger cities especially, are increasingly becoming professionalized. But a national network of schools would speed up the process and, hopefully, produce high-caliber police officers who today, because of Supreme Court decisions and the complexity of life itself, almost have to be lawyers first to be policemen secondarily.

Quite naturally, professionalization on a mass scale would demand higher pay scales for policemen. Still, the extra money expended by the public to this end would be more than worthwhile if the astronomical costs of crime each year were substantially cut.

To make another concession, education does not endow any man with an uncommon quality called common sense. Nevertheless, it might produce a policeman superior in many ways: superior in knowing precisely what his job is, what he must do to legally acquit the duties of his office, and what he must do in particularly delicate situations which require diplomacy and supremely good judgment on the part of the police officer precisely because he has enormous power which should be exercised judiciously.

The idea may be visionary, but a national police force would provide an army of policemen who, supported by the teeming millions of law-abiding citizens, could set up special task forces ready at a moment's notice to deter crime in high-crime areas and special riot-control units with the equivalency of military training, also ready to move on a moment's notice, even possibly being helicoptered into areas torn by riots, looting, and other mob-controlled lawlessness.

Right now in a New York State county police have been receiving special instruction in riot control. They have been issued rifles, shotguns, helmets, and other paraphernalia. Under consideration is a special vehicle completely enveloped in barbed wire, which, because of what it could do to human flesh, would very likely cause rioters to disperse or retreat before it. Still, despite these precautions, should riots suddenly flare up, the police are only equipped to fight a delaying action until the National Guard is summoned. The police have neither the force nor the equipment to do a total job.

National riot-control units composed of Federal and state forces as co-partners would obviate the need for this sort of partial protection against rioting. The whole setup would, however, be costly—nothing comes cheap in this world—and there would be the additional hazard that Washington, D. C. might want to dictate how the equivalent of a national police force should operate; but the states would still have the trump card, so to speak, by refusing to join in a "Compact on Crime" if the Federal Government sought to exercise dictatorial control.

Whether the dream of a national police force schooled to come to grips with crime in a nationwide basis is realized or not, there is no doubt that police forces are weak in many sections of the country. Even in New York City, more police are needed to augment the city's present 28,000-man force. John J. Cassese, head of the Patrolmen's Benevolent Association of the City of New York, said on a television program on December 12, 1966: "We should add 2,000 policemen to this police force, to be used solely for foot patrol. We sorely need men on the beat . . . men who deal with the people, who know the local conditions, who get to know conditions on their posts." The uniformed man walking up and down the street, he asserted, "would be a good deterrent to crime."

On the same program, Mr. Cassese also advocated a "get-tough" policy on the part of the police. Asked whether he was "worried that the policeman on the beat do not have the power to get tough," he replied: "Yes, under certain conditions. Surely, I don't expect every policeman (to get tough), and I don't say we should get tough just for the sake of getting tough . . . But I think you have to get tough if you're going to have law and order."

Mr. Cassese has scored light sentences given by the courts. Decrying the lack of attention accorded the victim of crime, he said: "When (criminals) do go to jail, they're released on good behavior, and they're right back at the same old crime . . . If you put them away for a long time, you'd cut crime in half."

Whether longer prison terms would indeed act as a deterrent may be debatable. Certain it is, though, that during his prison term, at least, the criminal cannot repeat any of his crimes in the outside world.

The dope pusher, as already recommended, should be dealt with severely. He's a mass murderer or the equivalent of a mass murderer who consigns his victims to a form of living death while they're able to survive and of course, to oblivion when survival no longer becomes possible. Giving the dope pusher a light sentence and the opportunity to "kill off" more victims when he is free again is not only against sound public policy; it goes against the grain of common sense.

As I view it, dope is really our number one national problem. Where on another day they may have sought escape in alcohol, many of our youth today, on college campuses especially, who can't face life, its problems and responsibilities, seek escape in dope. There are other possible reasons, of course, though they're still related to the inability to face life. Taking dope can even help a man dodge the draft.

We see many manifestations of the failure of the young to face life. Young men become girl-like in appearance and behavior possibly because they realize, consciously or unconsciously, that the female is exempted from war and from many other burdens of life that the man who is a man must face up to unflinchingly.

There are those who say dope is not a police matter; it's a medical matter. To this writer, it's basically neither: It's a moral matter. Look to a man's beginnings if you would truly know him. The boy or girl reared as an integral unit of a family wholesome in its living habits, religious in its beliefs, and dedicated to the proposition that only one kind of life, the moral life, is the right form of existence is not likely to stray into a life of crime. Or to seek escape from reality via dope.

With a national police force or at least beefed up police forces throughout the nation at the beck and call of a people standing four-square *behind* their police and *against* the forces of evil which breed crime, there yet remains one vital question: What good are our police or any police, for that matter, if a court like the U. S. Supreme Court continues to put what is tantamount to a premium on lawlessness while it in effect penalizes the victim rather than the perpetrator of crime?

We have seen what the criminal-protecting U. S. Supreme Court decisions have done to the cause of justice. They have made the criminal's rights superior to those of his victim. In so doing, have they meted out justice? How could they?

By hobbling the police, they make it easier for the criminal to get away with murder, rape, just plain thievery, or other crimes. And generally speaking, they give the criminal greater freedom than he has ever enjoyed before to prey upon the innocents, the victims of crime who are denied, to a certain extent, both the protections of the police and the protections of the judicial process.

The Honorable Norman J. Arterburn, Chief Justice of the Indiana Supreme Court, put the matter rather succinctly. Said he: "When an admitted, convicted criminal is freed by the courts on some technical ground which does not go to the merits of his guilt, there is something wrong with our judicial system."

There is a host of things wrong with the administration of justice in this country. And to correct the wrongs, we must start from the top down.

If we all stand equal under the law, as the Fourteenth Amendment to the U. S. Constitution implies, then the potential victim of crime should at least stand co-equal with the criminal insofar as the protections of the law are concerned. But the historic, criminal-pampering Supreme Court decisions mention the victims of crime sparingly, if at all. While they in effect legislate by setting forth rules and regulations for police departments to follow in the in-custody questioning of suspects, they do not utter so much as a single syllable about how the victim of crime may protect himself from the criminal.

When a six-person confessed murderer is freed on a U. S. Supreme

Court-prescribed technicality, how can the American people have ei
ther confidence in or respect for our system of "justice"?

Perhaps the Supreme Court of the United States, which, after all
like any governmental body in America, is, in the final analysis, an
swerable to the people, can answer that question. Here is one citizer
who seriously doubts it.

There is one overall question tacitly posed by the U. S. Supreme
Court decision. Should we, the people, willingly permit ourselves to be
victimized by the criminal simply because the court affords him better
protection than it does the law-abiding citizen?

The women from Orlando, Florida, seemingly don't think so. They
went out and bought arms and, through the courtesy of the local po
lice, learned how to use them. So any court-protected would-be rapis
who attacks one of those plucky women stands an excellent chance o
getting himself shot full of holes.

If the U. S. Supreme Court is genuinely the law-upholding body
it professes to be, maybe it will one day begin to recognize that al
U. S. citizens enjoy the right to life, liberty, and the pursuit of happi
ness, which is effectively denied them when they dare not walk the
streets at night for fear of their very lives. Contrariwise, the mass mur
derer given his liberty by the U. S. Supreme Court can, unlike the law
abiding citizen, enjoy life and pursue happiness in any way he pleases
including bumping off a couple of more people if the spirit so move
him. After all, if he can get away with mass murder, who not mas
mass murder?

In the last analysis, if the court won't protect the people, then th
people must, perforce, move to protect themselves from the court. W
can do that by insisting that Congress, our direct representatives, cli
the wings of the U. S. Supreme Court by curbing its appellate powers

Article III, Section 2, paragraph 2 of the U. S. Constitution says
"In all Cases affecting Ambassadors, other public Ministers and Con
suls, and those in which a State shall be Party, the Supreme Cour
shall have original Jurisdiction. In all the other Cases before men
tioned, the supreme Court shall have appellate Jurisdiction, both a
to Law and Fact, *with such Exceptions, and under such Regulation
as the Congress shall make.*" (Italics supplied.)

That section of the Constitution clearly clothes the Congress with
the power to regulate and control the appellate powers of the U. S
Supreme Court.

For its part, Congress is not exactly unmindful of its prerogative under this section. Back in the 1950's, Senator William E. Jenner introduced a bill which would have limited the Supreme Court's jurisdictional powers; and that bill failed of passage by only a few votes. Other congressmen have given this matter serious thought. Yet, despite the system of checks and balances built into the Constitution by its framers, the Court continues to act as a check on the legislative power, while the Congress, which has a similar constitutional right to act as a check on the Court, has never invoked that right.

It will indeed be a sad day if the Congress should curb the appelate powers of the "court of last resort." But if such an eventuality should ever come to pass, the blame will lie squarely on the shoulders of a court which has failed to afford equal protection of the laws to *all* the people of the United States. The people of this country do not like dictators in any shape or form—even dictators in black robes.

The conclusion is inescapable that model arrest, interrogation, arraignment, and prosecution codes are unachievable on a natonal basis, particularly since the arrest, indictment, and conviction of suspects may be completely nullified if U. S. Supreme Court-approved procedures aren't strictly abided by. Nonetheless, a move should be made in that direction.

Why couldn't the Federal Government get together with the states and draft such codes to make for procedural uniformity throughout the nation? Much of the spadework has already been done by the American Law Institute, the well-regarded private law-giver. It has drafted a model code of pre-arraignment procedure. While the preliminary draft contains some provisions which have effectively been knocked into a cocked hat by the Miranda decision, the ALI's experience in this field would prove an invaluable asset to Federal and state officials who got together to work out a "Compact on Crime."

In any event, for our very survival if for no more compelling reason, we must unhandcuff our police. We must help them do the job for which we hire them: to preserve law and order and to inceasingly battle crime and stamp it out wherever it is uncovered.

The job won't be easy; no worthwhile effort ever is. For as matters stand, we have essentially become a godless nation in a godless world. Crime increases as the religious influence wanes. We are in the midst of a social revolution when what is sorely needed is a moral revolution, which, if it ever got underway in earnest, would make the social revolution unnecessary.

Family life should be strengthened, bolstered, buttressed. Why, then, do so many forces in our society, including some agencies of government, do their uttermost to tear families apart? And why is God dead in the public schools of America? Shouldn't the moral law be taught in the schools?

As already substantially implied, there is no particular, no ready, no panacean answer to crime in America. If we are to win the war against crime, however, we must once more become a moral, not an amoral or immoral nation. If we would excise the cancer of crime which is eating the heart and soul out of our country, we must, all of us, return to the ways of the honest man, honest both with himself and with his God.

And, as stated before, as we return to Godliness, we must support those who support us: the policemen foresworn to meet crime on the field of human combat and to defeat it so that we who would return to the teachings of our fathers and their Godly ways may at least enter our houses of worship secure in the knowledge that no potential murderer, rapist, or thief lurks within their sacred portals. The alternative is to place a policeman in every church, just as New York City had to do with its subway trains during certain hours.

Again, in acting as the eyes and ears and in some cases even the nose of the policeman in helping wipe out crime, we citizens are not only upholding the law; we are waging war against the immoral monster in our midst.

Could organized or syndicated crime stand successfully against the policemen of the nation backed to the hilt by 100 million adults demanding the complete demolition of the "house of crime" in this land? I doubt it.

Did someone say we should police the police? Nonsense. Let's police America!